JACKSON HOLE

on a grand scale

BY

David Gonzales

FOREWORD

Pepi Stiegler

PHOTOGRAPHS

Wade McKoy

Bob Woodall

Jim Elder

Fletcher Manley

Carl Oksanen

David Gonzales

Greg von Doersten

Florence McCall

Chris Figenshau

Jonathan Selkowitz

John Layshock

Bruce Morley

Jeff Diener

David O'Connor

Bill Scott

Ted Wood

Andrew McGarry

Pepi Stiegler

MOUNTAIN SPORTS PRESS

Jackson Hole: On a Grand Scale

Published by
Mountain Sports Press
929 Pearl Street, Suite 200
Boulder, Colorado 80302

Distributed to the book trade by:
PUBLISHERS GROUP WEST

Design by Michelle Klammer Schrantz
Series Editor: Bill Grout

ISBN 0-9676747-3-5
Library of Congress Cataloging-in
Publication Data applied for.

Printed in Canada
By Friesens Corp.

This book is available from independent
and chain bookstores, online,
or by calling 303-448-7610.

To every skier and snowboarder
who moved to Jackson Hole for one winter
and never left.

Contents

In the early Sixties, while having dinner with a group of American skiers in the dining room of the Hotel Portillo in Portillo, Chile, Lucy Rockefeller, at the time unknown to me, engaged some of us at the table in a conversation about a place in Wyoming she described as paradise. She was talking about a place where there are the most beautiful mountains, beautiful lakes, a national park, thousands of elk, bear, and moose (I did not know what a moose was at the time) and all kinds of birds. Her description grabbed my attention and created a special image in my mind. Little did I know at the time what kind of impact that place would have on my life.

A year after the 1964 Olympics in Innsbruck, I received a call from Paul McCollister, the founder of the Jackson Hole Ski Resort. This was the most important phone call I ever received. After that call, my life was forever changed. I met Paul for the first time in the early summer of 1965 in Innsbruck in the Hotel Europa. Paul gave a presentation on Jackson Hole that no one has ever surpassed. It was the best sales job I ever heard in my life. Paul's narration was truthful and his enthusiasm was genuine. He offered me the ski school director's position at the new resort. I took my first trip to Jackson Hole in August of 1965, at Paul's invitation. We floated to the top of Rendezvous Mountain in a helicopter and hiked down. While doing so, we ran into two gigantic moose on what is now called Rendezvous trail. I have never seen bigger moose since that day.

I was awed by the beauty of this special place. I fell in love with it and took possession of it. This happened at a time when others had already discovered God's Country and claimed it for themselves. It appears that this is a perpetual cycle in Jackson Hole.

Only after some time, and after getting to know the place more thoroughly, was I able to really appreciate the privilege I was given. It took me a while to learn about the beauty of Jackson Hole in the summertime, because I spent my summers in Austria during the first few years. Jackson Hole turned out to be the perfect place for me. I was able to do what I like best, which is ski, and while doing so also make a good living. The job opportunity in Jackson Hole offered me an elevated station in life for which I am forever thankful to the owners of the resort.

I am also thankful to the members of the Jackson Hole Ski School. I have many fond memories. In the early days, there were the Austrian instructors that I personally handpicked: Peter Habeler, Erik Hotter, Peter Damit, Franz Ehrnsberger, Walter Perwein—he was the "bird man"; he and I were always flying over the catwalks—and Hias Tribuser, who still works as a ski instructor and mountain guide in Zürs, in the Arlberg. We paid them $400 per month. I remember we almost lost our Austrian instructors the first year the tram was open. They decided one day to ski down the north ridge of Rendezvous Mountain, which is strictly off-limits. They thought it looked like very good skiing. Mountain Manager Gordy Wren almost fired them. But I suppose Paul McCollister told him he couldn't do that—we needed them to teach.

By 1973, we could no longer hire the Austrians; the U.S. immigration had begun to crack down on giving visas to foreign ski instructors. They added some flair to the place, but I am most proud of the instructors who came later. I was an intense director, very demanding, but I gave them very good training and several went far. There was Toni Hardy, who moved on to become ski school director at Squaw Valley, California; Bob Barnes, who became a member of the PSIA Demo Team and later ski school director at Park City, Utah, Crystal Mountain, Washington, and Winter Park, Colorado;

Victor Gerdin, my assistant ski school director, who also became a member of the Demo Team and later the ski school director at Snowmass, Colorado; and Pat Campbell. Pat started as an apprentice ski instructor in our school and eventually became our first female assistant ski school director. She moved on to run the ski school at Grand Targhee Ski Resort and eventually became director of the ski school at Breckenridge. Now she's in an upper management position at Breckenridge.

There are many other instructors who are important to me: Renny Burke, the cowboy and rancher who has been teaching at Jackson Hole since the second year, Richard Lee, Vern Peterson, Susan Hedden, Billy Dciezic, Jamie Macintosh, Lexey Waters, and Theo Meiners. When some of our longtime customers return for their annual vacation at Teton Village, they expect to see Renny, Richard, Susan, Vern, and Billy. Jackson Hole Mountain Resort would not be the same without them.

It has been thirty-six years since I came here, and the place still holds a strong fascination for me. It is my belief that Jackson Hole harbors the most alluring ski mountain in the country. I consider my two children exceptionally privileged to be natives here, to grow up in this special place and become so intimate with the sport of skiing.

The mountain, in the early days, was like paradise. Has it lost its charm and character? Charm is a very personal matter and relative to an individual's perception. As far as the quality of the skiing, I must say it has changed for the better. In the late 1980s, there were resort customers who told us we should give them a call when we replaced our old lifts for newer and faster ones. The lift facilities have been drastically improved, so has the snowmaking (there was none in the early years), not to mention slope grooming. The quality of summer and winter grooming has made the mountain more accessible to a larger segment of the skiing population. With the arrival of shorter, shaped skis, the mountain feels more tame and easier to handle. The ski industry's advances in technology have made our mountain a better one.

Pepi Stiegler

Should we ever forget how special a place Jackson Hole really is, then we only need listen to our national and international visitors. They will straighten us out and confirm what we felt when we first came here. Some of our customers tell me with conviction that when the snow conditions are right, Jackson Hole is the best ski mountain they know of.

David Gonzales has put into this important book a great deal of effort, research, and much time. He deserves a lot of credit for this accomplishment. Jackson Hole's winter history means so much to those of us who have worked and played here for the better part of our lives. His book describes Jackson Hole's authentic ski culture as nobody has done before. His chapters permit us to relive the years long past. The stories in this book confirm to those of us who have been here since the beginning that we are very privileged. As time passes, everything will change; therefore we can be grateful for what we have experienced here. Do I regret leaving the Austrian Alps for the Grand Tetons? Never.

Enjoy!

February 11, 6:07 A.M.

The phone's keypad glows in the dark as I dial the number for the Jackson Hole Mountain Resort's morning snow report. "Six inches of new snow in the last twenty-four hours," says the recording. Outside the window, fresh pillows of snow crown fence posts and shrubs. Waves of flakes halo the streetlights. The sky wears the slightest tinge of blue. The report, taken from an automatic gauge high on Rendezvous Mountain, has been stingy all season. Instead of six inches, there could be eight. Or ten. Sleeping any longer is out of the question.

On the road to Teton Village, I pass a herd of horses moving across a pasture in the predawn gloom. They plod in single file, their backs dusted white.

At 7:15 A.M., one hour and forty-five minutes before the resort opens, the tram maze at the village already sprouts a thicket of skis and poles. The protocol: If you arrive early—by seven—you can leave your skis in line while you buy a breakfast burrito or warm up in Nick Wilson's restaurant. Don't return to your spot much later than eight, however, or you might find your skis tossed over the rail into the snow thirty feet below.

But if you're unwilling to stake out a place in line, you're missing the point. Arriving early enough for "first box" is as much about the buzz as it is about the snow. First box doesn't necessarily mean first tracks. After all, the ski area opens to the public only after several tram-loads of patrollers, guides, instructors, clients, photographers, models, and a few smooth talkers have already unloaded atop the mountain. But it does mean fresh tracks, as well as a fresh chance to bond with others in line who share your disease.

Call it Rendezvous fever. It's marked by insomnia (many in the tram line woke before their alarm clocks rang), numbness (the body's natural defense when standing in the frigid tram dock for two or more hours), and restlessness (only on a powder day does 9 A.M. seem like a long time in coming).

The disease is particularly virulent among young Jacksonites, but its range is far wider. First in line this

The bigger the powder day, the earlier you have to arrive at the tram dock to get a place in the first box.

morning is a group of five from California. "We live in San Diego," one of them says. He nods to their ringleader, who perches on the barricade closest to the turnstile. "Actually, *he* lives in Jackson; he just visits San Diego 360 days a year."

The ringleader grins and shrugs. He woke his companions up at 6:00 this morning to be at the tram at 6:30. "I fell in love with this place the first time I came, in 1973," he says. On that trip, it snowed three feet one morning; he was one of only eight skiers on first box.

Times have changed. It's 8:15, and the maze at the tram dock is completely full. Outside the maze, all the neophytes who thought they'd get first box by arriving forty-five minutes early mill about helplessly, like sheep on the wrong side of the fence, cut off from the rest of the flock. Inside the maze, rumors abound of snowfall twice as deep as what was reported. Previous powder days are relived. Plans for the day's first runs are mulled

over. You can bet everybody knows exactly where they will head once they've unloaded at the top. But don't bet on them telling you.

Nine A.M. finally arrives. "Have your passes and lift tickets ready!" Fifty-four skiers and boarders file through the turnstile and crowd into the tramcar. It leaves the dock, floating for the summit. Conversation dwindles. Everybody studies the mountain as it slips past, drinking in with their eyes what they will soon consume with their feet. Near the upper tram dock, the attendant's radio crackles with an order from ski patrol: "You're going to have to hold that car at the top. Don't open the doors."

Everybody groans. But when the tram stops, the doors fly open. A cold wind leaps into the car, and the tram dock rumbles under 108 heavy boots. Despite the patrol's protests, the eager occupants of the first box have been unleashed onto the mountain. They clatter down the metal stairs, throw skis and snowboards onto the snow, and shove boots into bindings. A minute later, the mountain's summit is silent again, save for the whirring of the tram's haul cable as the car heads back down. From below, in Rendezvous Bowl, come the whoops and howls of paradise found.

chapter 1

THE AMAZING TETONS

A RANGE OF POSSIBILITIES

"These are the first mountains I've seen that look like mountains should look."

So said President Theodore Roosevelt, supposedly, the first time he saw the Tetons. Even if Roosevelt never said such a thing, many have thought it. In their steepness, their abruptness, and the way they advance in height from the range's northern and southern ends toward the Grand Teton's stark, triangular climax, the Tetons seem to have been designed with hyperbole in mind. Stand nearly anywhere on Jackson Hole's valley floor and look west: There they are in all their splendor, arrayed in a row beyond the sagebrush, every summit, snowfield, and precipice in view. How bold. How unabashed. How American. Perhaps this is what struck Roosevelt—it's as if the American spirit, in all its ambition and bombast, has been etched on the landscape itself.

And yet this is only a two-dimensional view of the Tetons, the one most tourists see while driving from the wooden sidewalks of Jackson to the wooden walkways of Yellowstone's Old Faithful Geyser Basin. To turn off the road into Teton Village or into Grand Teton National Park, pull on one's ski or hiking boots, and venture into these formidable peaks is to be drawn into a multidimensional world. One of breadth. Of complexity. Of canyons, lakes, and crags invisible to those who remain on Highway 191 or the Moose-Village Road. Gazing at the Tetons from the valley floor, one wants to gush, as Roosevelt did. Exploring the Tetons, however, one resists turning thoughts into words.

The interior of the Tetons is, put simply, paradise. Its gates are the glacially carved canyons that incise the range at regular intervals: Granite, Open, Death, Avalanche, Garnet, and Cascade, among others. At their mouths, tall pines lean over noisy creeks. At their heads, two or three thousand feet higher, lonely, crenelated cirques cup small, icy lakes. In between the canyons' mouths and the highest reaches live black bears, grizzlies, moose, elk, marmots, weasels, and goshawks, their lives among the dark walls hardly disturbed by humans. In the summer, Cascade and Death Canyons see steady streams of hikers, and some high meadows suffer frequent outbreaks of bright nylon blisters (i.e., tents). But by autumn these are gone. In the winter, snow obliterates all trails and campsites, muffles all sounds but the wind, and with each storm wipes clean the ski tracks that are the only human signatures on the high peaks for seven months of the year.

14

The Cathedral Group of the Tetons, in a perspective first made famous by Ansel Adams.

Above: The Tetons, seen through a window in the Joe Pfeiffer Homestead. Joe Pfeiffer, born in 1878, built the homestead between 1910 and 1916. It burned in a range fire in 1994. Right: One of three signs greeting visitors to the valley. This one, on Teton Pass, was erected in the mid-1930s, and recently replaced with an exact replica on the opposite side of the road.

The winters in Jackson Hole are infamous. Credit the snowstorms that lash western Wyoming from October to April for having kept the Tetons and the adjacent eastward valley pristine. Until the turn of the twentieth century, nobody lived year-round in Jackson Hole (so called because early trappers called an area encircled by mountains a hole, rather than a valley, which is only flanked by mountains). Despite the depictions in Jackson's art galleries, Indians did not gather around their teepees in the snow, the Grand Teton looming overhead. Rather, the first native Americans who came to the Tetons ten thousand years ago and all those who followed—the warlike Blackfeet and Gros Ventres, the peaceable Shoshones and Bannocks—spent only summers here. Or they did not pause at all, using the valley merely as a corridor.

The mountain men, such pivotal figures in Jackson Hole's lore, also preferred more hospitable wintering grounds. Like the Indians, they left little physical evidence of their passing in the early 1800s, but they did leave a few important names, such as that of an American, Davey Jackson, who particularly liked hunting here. French trappers left us "Les Trois Tetons," the three breasts, which

Above: The White Grass Ranch, near the present-day Death Canyon trailhead in Grand Teton National Park, was in operation between 1919 and 1985. Left: John Carnes (with beard), one of the first three settlers in Jackson Hole, flanked by his half-brother Bud Serose (at left) and Bob Jackson. The photo was taken in 1884, the year Carnes arrived in Jackson Hole.

refer to the view of the peaks from the western side. This is at least a more poetic name than that offered by an early party of American trappers, who dubbed the peaks "the Pilot Knobs."

By 1840, the fur trade had all but dried up, as silk rather than beaver hats became the latest fashion. In the next half century, a few expeditions came west to scout, map, and hunt the area, including the famous U.S. Geographical Survey of the Territories (better known as the Hayden Survey of 1872).

Two members of this survey, Langford and Stevenson, claimed they reached the summit of the Grand Teton while exploring the range. This was fiercely disputed by William Owen, who claimed the first ascent, with three others, in 1898. The debate over who first climbed the monarch of the Tetons still smolders.

What is more certain is the date of arrival of Jackson Hole's first permanent settlers—trapper John Holland, his friend John Carnes, and Carnes's Indian wife, Millie—who came in 1884. Descending into the valley from the Gros Ventre Range to the east, the trio homesteaded on Flat Creek, now within the National Elk Refuge. More settlers soon trickled in to make their livings as farmers, ranchers, and hunting guides.

Believe what you will about Jackson's image as the "last of the old West"—tourism has existed here as long as the town itself. The first tourists were big-game hunters from the East, who came right on the heels of the first settlers. They were soon joined by another form of visitor: the dude. In 1908, Louis Joy established Jackson Hole's first dude ranch, the JY Ranch on Phelps Lake (in present-day Grand Teton National Park). The trade quickly took hold, as struggling ranchers found it easier to exploit the striking Teton scenery than the valley's windswept grazing lands.

The JY Ranch is historic in another sense; owned by the Rockefeller family since the 1920s (and recently donated to the park), it reflects the successful efforts of John D. Rockefeller, Jr., to save much of the valley floor from commercial development. When Grand Teton National Park was established in 1929, it included only the Teton peaks and the small lakes at their feet. About the same time, Rockefeller, who deplored the hot-dog stands and filling stations that had sprung up around Jenny Lake, began buying nearby properties with the intent to donate them to the new park. He did it in secret, so ranchers and farmers

An Array of Light. Left to Right: the Cathedral Group
(with the Grand Teton in clouds), Mount St. John, Mount Woodring, and Mount Moran.

wouldn't arbitrarily raise their prices when they heard whom they were dealing with. Inevitably, word got out, infuriating residents and Wyoming lawmakers. It was not until 1950 that tempers calmed enough for Rockefeller's lands to be added to the park.

To the south, not far from the JY Ranch, the park dips into glacially carved Granite Canyon, then climbs sharply to its boundary on the crest of a broad peak crowned by massive golden cliffs. Not antic-

ipating its future importance to locals and visitors, the U.S. Geological Survey gave this mountain the prosaic name of Peak 10,450, for its height in feet. Now we know it as Rendezvous Mountain, the center-piece of Jackson Hole Mountain Resort. (In 1998, Jackson Hole Ski Resort changed its name to Jackson Hole Mountain Resort.)

Rendezvous Mountain is actually an outlier of pyramidal Rendezvous Peak, which is three miles to the south and a few hundred feet higher. The entire massif is sedimentary, meaning it's still clad in the seaborne rock that glaciers and erosion have stripped from the spires in the park itself. But it's not as rounded as the mountains farther south. In other words, Rendezvous Mountain occupies the ideal position in the Teton

Range for a ski resort—it's steep and complex like the peaks in the national park, but not so steep that it can't be skied or hold snow. And hold snow it does—25 to 40 feet of the stuff falls on Rendezvous Mountain every winter, with some high, shady patches remaining until August.

Long before snow brought skiers, gold brought miners to Rendezvous Mountain. Because Jackson Hole was unknown and so far from railroads, few prospectors came north from Colorado during that state's gold-mining glory days. One who did was Jim Fleming, who sold his claim to the Molly Gibson vein in Aspen and came north to Wyoming in the 1890s. Joined by a brother from Missouri, Fleming

prospected in the southern Tetons, striking gold directly in the middle of what is now Jackson Hole Mountain Resort.

"It was a high grade of ore," says George Fleming, Jim's grand-nephew, who still lives at the base of the Tetons. "He had different claims staked all over, and he'd go up there and work in the summer."

In relation to modern landmarks, the Fleming's main shaft was just to the northeast of Thunder Lift's upper station. More diggings

Left, Rendezvous Mountain (officially, Peak 10,450) before lifts. Top: Jim Fleming, the prospector of Rendezvous Mountain. Bottom: Nineteenth-century hunting parties liked to pose with their trophies. Below: George Fleming, grand-nephew of Jim Fleming and first employee of Jackson Hole Ski Corporation.

lay on a rocky slope just south of the Aerial Tram's tower three. Today this slope, usually closed to skiers, bears the appropriate name Gold Miner's.

George Fleming, whose father ran away from his home in Anaconda, Montana, to help his uncles with their Teton gold mine, was born at the base of Rendezvous Peak. In 1964, he was given a chance to follow in his father's and great-uncles' footsteps when Jackson Hole Ski Resort founders Paul McCollister and Alex Morley made him their first employee. Hired to bulldoze a road up Rendezvous in advance of the tram's construction, Fleming wandered into an area known as the Cirque. He remembered his father had told him that somewhere in the vicinity was his great-uncles' mining camp.

Above: The Tetons in early summer. Right: The first coyotes didn't appear in
Jackson Hole until the twentieth century, after the eradication of the wolf.

"It was kind of a funny deal, eerie," recalls Fleming. "I'd never
been up there, but I knew exactly where to go. I found the old camp, then
walked up and found the old mine shaft just like I'd been there a hundred
times before."

His great-uncles had hoped to put a stamp mill in the Cirque,
where there was a small lake, later obliterated by a landslide. To transport
gold to their homestead below, they planned to build an ore tram.

"So Paul McCollister and Alex Morley weren't the first ones who
thought about a tram on Rendezvous Mountain," says Fleming. "My
uncles were going to disassemble it, pack it up on horses. But Jim got
killed or died before he ever got started on it."

Meanwhile, a small community of farmers were living below

Rendezvous Peak, on the land now occupied
by Teton Village. Theirs was an onerous life of
long winters spent waiting for a woefully short
growing season. Incomes were paltry. Few
homesteaders could afford to patent, or "prove
up," their properties, which would have meant
legally gaining ownership of the land from the
U.S. government.

"In those days you homesteaded
and then didn't prove up for ten or fifteen
years," said lifelong Jackson resident
Rex Ross in a 1972 interview. Like George

View from the Walton Ranch, which was assembled by oilfield geologist Paul Walton in 1959. Before he died in 1998, Walton protected the ranch's open vistas with a conservation easement.

Hole naturalists, biologists, authors, and conservationists. "So biologically it's not that unusual to see grizzlies in the southern Tetons. Now that they've had some protection, they're able to occupy territory they occupied thirty or forty years ago."

Grizzlies, as any hiker who has ever tied bear bells to his backpack knows, are at the top of the food chain. Each step of that chain is well represented at Jackson Hole Mountain Resort, which, because it abuts Grand Teton National Park, is nearly as wild as the park itself.

Moose and elk, for instance, are often found wandering the lower reaches of the resort. Since Jackson Hole was settled in the late 1800s, elk hunting has been a mainstay of the local economy. It's also had various impacts on the natural world, evident at the ski resort. As hunting pressures have pushed the elk south and west, for example, some of the animals have begun wintering around the resort rather than migrating to the National Elk Refuge on the eastern side of the valley. Also, elk-gut piles left by hunters have caused an increase in ravens, frequently seen wheeling in the winter sky over the ski slopes, as well as bald and golden eagles, which normally migrate elsewhere in cold weather.

This, of course, is bad news for the raptors' prey: squirrels, deer mice, muskrats, and voles. Some of these ski-area inhabitants already have their own clever defenses in place; ermine, for instance, turn completely white except for their tails' black tips. The ground squirrel hibernates, his body temperature dropping from ninety-seven to thirty-nine degrees Fahrenheit, and his heart rate dropping from 250 to ten beats per minute. Also hibernating for the winter is the yellow-bellied marmot, the self-appointed sentinel of the Tetons' high crags and boulder fields. Take a hike from the

On the Wild Side

Two bull moose square off at Blacktail Ponds, Grand Teton National Park

I n late April 2001, an archery hunter killed a grizzly bear near Jackson Hole Mountain Resort. It was almost certainly an honest mistake, as the hunter thought he was taking a legal shot at a black bear. This was the first grizzly seen in the ski area's vicinity in more than two decades.

Grizzlies, it has long been thought, keep to the northern reaches of Grand Teton National Park, where trails—and, therefore, people—are rare. But this incident shows that grizzlies, protected under the Endangered Species Act, are expanding their range to the south. According to naturalist Derek Craighead, who runs Beringia South, a research and education nonprofit organization, this may mean we're going to see more grizzlies around the ski resort and Teton Village.

"Up to fifty years ago, before most of them were trapped, shot, or poisoned, grizzlies were common all through the Teton range," says Craighead, who is part of the well-known Craighead clan of Jackson

aerial tram in the summer, and you'll almost certainly see a marmot, or at least hear his high-pitched warning chirp.

What you probably won't see—summer or winter—are the Tetons' more secretive species: wolverines (small, bearlike creatures with long tails), bighorn sheep, and mountain lions. And though they're seen rarely in the Tetons, mountain lions, thinks Craighead, may very well roam the ski area.

"They're in all areas around it," he says. "They're in the Gros Ventre Mountains, in the Snake River Canyon, on Blacktail Butte, and in the Beaver Creek area within a few miles of Teton Village. They're secretive and somewhat nocturnal, so they're not likely to be seen, but there's no reason they wouldn't be there."

Mountain lions, grizzlies, wolverines, bald eagles—how many ski areas can boast such inhabitants? Even if one disregards Rendezvous Mountain's daunting ski terrain or the audacity of its skiers and snowboarders, Jackson Hole could still be called the wildest ski resort in the world.

Fleming, Ross also grew up on a homestead below Rendezvous Peak. "In order to prove up," said Ross, "you had to live on it and have so much improvements, and then come up with $116, which was a lot of money."

On May 28, 1921, Harry Spalding, who grew up on the JY Ranch, patented an eighty-acre homestead on Rendezvous's lower slopes. Shaded by quaking aspens and ribboned with streams, many of which gurgled right from the ground on the property, the Crystal Springs Ranch would eventually become Teton Village. But for the first eight years, the property belonged to Spalding, whom Ross called "the meanest little man in the world."

In 1929, Spalding sold his homestead, which by then totaled about 159 acres, to Hiram Harrison. The ranch changed hands several more times before it was purchased by Ken Clatterbaugh and his wife, Shirley, who transformed the Crystal Springs Ranch into a girl's camp.

According to Marilyn Kruecke, a counselor at the camp in 1950 and 1951, "Ken was not a very good businessman, and the ranch barely kept afloat financially. . . . He could barely pay his counselors, and the campers often rode newly broken ranch horses."

However raw their steeds, the campers ranged far and wide on horseback, riding to Moose for church services at the Chapel of the

Above: Crystal Springs Ranch, precursor to Teton Village, photographed in the early-1950s by wrangler Bill Scott, who now runs the horseriding concession at Teton Village. Right: Crystal Springs campers and counselors mounted and ready for a trail ride.

Transfiguration, to Wilson for the rodeo (some campers even participated), and to Jackson, where the girls would take in a movie before remounting their horses, "singing songs all the way back to the ranch."

By 1961, when Paul McCollister bought an option to purchase Clatterbaugh's property for the Jackson Hole ski resort, the Tetons and Jackson Hole were a well-known tourist attraction. Dude ranches were scattered throughout the area. Grand Teton National

Park was attracting nearly a million visitors per year. Every significant summit in the Tetons had been climbed, the Grand Teton alone by nearly forty separate technical routes.

But all this took place in the summer. Each autumn, the tourist business died. The story goes that Jackson restaurant owners flipped coins to decide who'd stay open for the winter. Many residents left. Those who lacked the means to do so, or who liked the quiet, stayed. Temperatures dropped, roads closed, lakes froze, and the elk wandered out of the high country. Before long, the mountains, valley, and town all were buried deeply under the winter's most abundant, least utilized resource. ❧

Uncle Nick Wilson

To properly impart a sense of history to the place, Nick Wilson's, the restaurant at the base of Jackson Hole Mountain Resort, ought to serve "lumpydick." A bland porridge made by boiling moistened flour in milk, lumpydick was one of the things that drove Elijah "Nick" Wilson, the restaurant's namesake and founder of the nearby town of Wilson, to his storied life of adventure.

Nick, who was born in Illinois in 1842, spent his early childhood on his Mormon family's small homestead in Utah. While tending his father's sheep herd, he passed the time by learning the Gosiute language from an Indian boy. A band of Shoshones camped nearby were delighted he could speak with them—the chief's mother had dreamt one of her dead sons would return as a white child and thought Nick could be that child if tempted away. So the Shoshones offered him all the fish, sage chickens, ducks, geese, and rabbits he could eat, plus a beautiful pinto pony, if he would come with them. "I thought this surely beat herding sheep and living on greens and lumpydick," he wrote in his famous autobiography, *Uncle Nick Among the Shoshonis*. Nick agreed to run away and, a few days later, found himself wearing buckskins, riding with the Shoshones, and answering to the name of Yagaiki. He was eleven years old.

Nick lived with the Shoshones for two years. He hunted buffalo, watched Chief Washakie and his warriors do battle with the Crows, and grew close to his "dear old Indian mother." But Nick's father, it was feared, would eventually come after him, so Nick returned home. He never went back to his Shoshone family, as he had hoped, but his exploits were hardly over.

A few years later, he answered the Pony Express ad, which called for "young, skinny wiry fellows, not over 18. Must be expert riders, willing to risk death daily. Orphans preferred."

Nick Wilson

In the course of his duties, which lasted about a year and a half, he was captured by Indians and subsequently let go, then shot by an arrow just above the left eye. The wound left him with a deep scar that he covered with a hat for the rest of his life.

As a grown man, Nick continued to wander, driving stagecoaches for the Overland Stage for a short while, serving as an Army scout and Indian interpreter, and working various jobs, from blacksmith to frontier doctor to prison guard. Finally in 1890, remembering his Indian brother Chief Washakie's tales of the fertile hunting grounds by the Yam-Pah-Pa River (Snake River), Nick led the first of several caravans of settlers into Jackson Hole. On one such caravan, it took twenty-eight days for the settlers to move their wagons and livestock the eighteen miles over Teton Pass. Nick himself settled in Jackson Hole soon afterward, finally establishing a homestead beside Fish Creek, near the base of the Tetons, in 1895. Building a hotel, livery stable, and Jackson Hole's first store on his property, he inspired others to build a school house, Mormon meeting house, and baseball diamond nearby. And so the town of Wilson was born, presided over by the legendary "Uncle" Nick until his death in 1915 at the age of seventy-three.

SKIING IN JACKSON HOLE: 1880s TO 1950s

FIRST TRACKS

Of all the landmarks in and around Jackson Hole—the Grand Teton, Jackson Lake, Yellowstone's Old Faithful Geyser—none has influenced the local population's rough-hewn character as much as Teton Pass, the notch in the southern Tetons rising 2,400 feet above the town of Wilson.

Today Teton Pass is little more than the crest of a long hill, climbed daily by commuters who've fled Jackson Hole for cheaper rents in Idaho. For some it's also a favorite place to embark on a backcountry ski tour. But in the early days, the pass was the valley's only effective link to the outside world. Togwotee Pass, Mosquito Creek Pass, and Hoback Canyon were negotiable only by foot or horse. When Teton Pass was blocked, as happened often in winter, the valley was sealed.

For outlaw settlers like horse rustler Teton Jackson and bandit Ed Trafton—whose specialty was holding up stagecoaches in Yellowstone National Park—the valley's remoteness was a boon. For more law-abiding citizens, however, the isolation was a constant challenge, overcome only by pluck and persistence. Take, for instance, a notice on the front page of the February 10, 1916, *Jackson's Hole Courier*, the valley's principal newspaper from 1909 to 1961:

"Because the [Oregon Short Line] trains have been unable to get through the snow and because we were unluckily caught with no supply of paper is not reason sufficient to keep the *Courier* from coming out on time. The merchants have come to the rescue with the last bit of wrapping paper in the valley and in case the mail does not arrive before the next issue, they have been kind enough to offer several rolls of paper. We think, however, that there will probably be paper here in time for the next issue as the stage drivers from both sides are making a big effort to get to the top of the pass. When you consider that five feet of new snow fell during the past two days on the pass, their task looks like a hard one."

Clearing the pass was crucial. On the far side lay the Oregon Short Line railhead, at St. Anthony, Idaho, the Jacksonites' most convenient supply point, though convenience is a relative term. The eighty-eight-mile stagecoach journey from Jackson to St. Anthony took two days, with eighteen hours of actual travel. In the summer, the rocky track punished wagons and horses. In the winter, the journey by sleigh was smoother but

On skis above Polecat Creek, at the southern boundary of Yellowstone National Park. In the distance, steam rises from Huckleberry Hot Springs.

less certain, thanks to heavy snow and frequent avalanches. Jackson Hole's inhabitants knew well that they could be shut off from civilization for weeks at a time.

But the deep snow and profound solitude were also catalysts, precipitating a way to move across snow that transcended mere transportation. To fetch supplies, visit friends, and fend off boredom, settlers took up skiing. It's impossible to name Jackson Hole's first skier. It may have been a pioneer, looking for the easiest way to travel among the nascent hamlets of Moran, Moose, and Elk; it may even have been John Colter, who wandered through the valley in the dead of winter in 1806 after leaving Lewis and Clark's expedition. In any case, as historic photographs

show, settlers had embraced skiing by the turn of the century, and Jacksonites have been honing their techniques and tools ever since.

By modern standards, the pioneers' skis needed some refinement. Hand-carved of red fir or lodgepole pine and measuring up to eight feet in length, they were unwieldy beasts. Ski wax didn't exist (though some early skiers experimented with honey, pine tar, and axle grease); bindings consisted of leather straps or boots nailed to the ski; and skiers used one

Left: Eugene Gillette (behind truck) and brother Francis Gillette assist a tanker of Pep 88 gasoline over Teton Pass. Above: Early local skiers Fred Brown, Betty Mueller, and Willy Mueller on Teton Pass, probably in the 1930s. Right: The journey over Teton Pass with horse-drawn sleds took a minimum of two days.

pole instead of two. To move across the flats, a skier handled his pole like a canoe paddle. To brake on descents, he dragged his pole between his legs.

Just as in the Colorado Rockies and California's Sierra Nevada, the first serious downhill skiers in the Tetons were mail carriers. Before the U.S. Postal Service would serve the valley, residents had to deliver the mail themselves, on schedule, for a year. Taking turns, the pioneers skied the mail back and forth

from Victor, Idaho, and were duly awarded with a post office. Located on the homestead of postmistress Mary White Tuttle, the aptly named Marysvale post office was the valley's first official institution and the kernel for the town of Jackson.

In a letter written almost sixty years later, White Tuttle recalled making a winter mail trip over the pass: "That ski trip is one thing I will never forget. Going up that hill, especially the last pitch, took some very skillful sidestepping straight up. It took us all forenoon and we stopped for lunch in the mail carrier's little snow cabin, or should I say 'igloo,' at the top of the pass. . . . It was easier going down the other side!"

In time, sleigh traffic on the pass became reliable, and mail carriers

"Jackson Hole Snow Conditions Termed Ideal for Skiing Purposes"

BY FRITZ BROWN

FROM *THE JACKSON'S HOLE COURIER*, DECEMBER 31, 1936

It is immensely gratifying to see so many good ski outfits skooting over the trails since Christmas. Good skiing is difficult without good equipment and unquestionably there are many times more well equipped skiers in Jackson Hole this winter than ever before. America's sudden and wholesale acceptance of modern skiing as a major sport, making good skiing the "thing," has put skis on our feet. Now let's use them!

We don't need to be told that our valley is the finest place in the West to live, that our mountains and our wildlife are incalculable spiritual and financial assets, and we don't hesitate to brag about them to our less fortunate friends from other regions. But discussions of the joys of winter have been conspicuous by their scarcity. Too many of us have ended lamely with the explanation that we can easily go outside when the snow begins to fly.

In Europe the Swiss dwelt happily in their mountains, enduring the rigors of winter for the sake of the heavenly summers and the freedom that their highlands preserved. It took strangers to show them first the wonders of their own land on skis. Must we, too, wait to be shown?

Anyone can learn to get around on skis in a short time. If he will be content to leave racing to the few. Ordinary skiing, touring, it is called, is not overly difficult and really requires no special knowledge or technique. A little acquaintance with the fundamentals of level running, climbing steps and low-speed turns will greatly facilitate the first few weeks progress, but once

Dressed to ski: Kay Willard Benson and Donald Naegli on Snow King, probably in the late-1940s.

this knowledge has been drilled into the legs, one is as well prepared for ski touring, up and down hills and through the flats, as for hikes and outings in the summer.

Many will be anxious to branch out from this modest beginning. The jumping hill, the slalom course, downhill racing, the lauglauf (cross country race) or ski mountaineering—each is highly specialized sport for the trained and advanced skier. Our hills and valleys afford perfectly marvelous opportunities for every branch of the sport. No mountains in the entire West are better adapted to winter mountaineering than the Tetons and the Grovonts. For most of us, the more strenuous types of skiing will remain things to exclaim over, but touring is for everyone. The line between skiing up a butte and ski mountaineering may be an indefinite one. An experienced tourist may run as swiftly home as a racer. But the oldest and the youngest among us can tour. Down with "cabin fever"! Let's get out on the snow.

Above: An unidentified racer on Snow King. Right: Neil Rafferty, father of lift-served skiing in Jackson Hole, with the rope tow he ran on Teton Pass each winter in the early season from the late 1940s to the late 1960s. The front and rear wheels each drove a set of ropes.

no longer had to carry Jackson Hole's correspondence or mail-order goods from Montgomery Ward on their backs. Skiing the pass mutated from chore to sport, as a few Jackson and Wilson residents began practicing downhill runs on the perfectly pitched slopes above the Trail Creek drainage and on Mount Glory. Thus was initiated a backcountry ski tradition on Teton Pass that still thrives today.

Most Jacksonites, however, took up the sport on the mountain directly above town, which was swept of trees by an 1879 forest fire. Called variously Kelly's Hill, the Ruth Hannah Simms Ski Hill, and simply "the town hill," the mountain is now named Snow King and is the cradle of lift-served skiing in Jackson Hole. The first lifts, however, came long after Snow King's first skiers, who climbed the hill for each run. These athletes may have lacked lifts, advanced ski equipment, and modern technique, but they didn't lack guts.

"Everybody around here in the early thirties was just going to the top of the hill and coming straight down and trusting to a bit of ability and a heck of a lot of luck," recalled Neil Rafferty, whose passion for skiing would infect countless townspeople. "Or they were building a jump somewhere and trying to ride over it. Jumping was the big kick then."

Racers gather at the starting gate atop Snow King in the 1940s.

In 1936, when the Civilian Conservation Corps completed a zigzagging horse and hiking trail to the top of Snow King, most skiers still could not turn. In the first ski race down the CCC trail, competitors stopped at each switchback or crashed into the bushes.

Says Rafferty of one of his competitors, who had careened off the racecourse: "He looked like he'd been in a fight with a bobcat. His face was all scratched, and the blood was a-runnin'. Just as he came out of the bushes, I came to the turn and seeing him scared the socks off of me."

Jackson Hole did not remain long in skiing's stone age. The sport's new era would be ushered in, appropriately, on Teton Pass. In 1937, the recently established Jackson Ski Club invited the Dartmouth

ski team to town. To a crowd of two hundred gathered on Telemark Bowl, near the top of the pass, Olympian Dick Durrance and his teammates demonstrated the use of modern ski equipment and technique.

Also in the 1930s, the Engen brothers, Alf and Sverre, came to Jackson to put on a jumping exhibition. (Big air, it seems, has always been in style at Jackson Hole.) But the greatest crowd pleasers may have been Wyoming's own "Hoback Boys," a foursome n 1937 the most famous skier in the U.S. was the young, dashing racer from Dartmouth College, Dick Durrance. National champion in the slalom, downhill, and alpine combined, Durrance had led the U.S. Olympic team to the 1936 Winter Games at Garmisch-Partenkirchen, Germany. But he'd never seen the Rockies—until Jackson Hole Ski Association President Fred Brown invited Durrance and his Dartmouth teammates to spend their Christmas holiday at Brown's Teton Pass Ranch. The purpose of the trip: to train for an upcoming series of races at Sun Valley against the University of Washington ski team.

"That was my first time west," recalls Durrance, now eighty-seven and living in Carbondale, Colorado. "We came out on the train. We thought the mountains in Jackson Hole were pretty goddamned big, compared to the East."

If Durrance and his teammates were impressed with the Tetons, the town of Jackson was just as impressed with them. For three weeks in a row, the *Jackson's Hole Courier* accorded their visit front-page coverage. DICK DURRANCE AND FAMOUS DARTMOUTH SKI TEAM TO SPEND CHRISTMAS IN JACKSON HOLE, reads the headline of a December 9 article. DARTMOUTH SKI TEAM TO PRACTICE ON TETON PASS, blares the December 23 issue. It was the first time anybody had come to Jackson Hole just to ski.

And ski they did, heading daily to the wide slopes on either side of Teton Pass. According to Durrance, "We hiked up everything—Mount Glory, everything on the other side of the pass. There was a whole batch of us. Me, Steve and David Bradley, John Litchfield, Warren and Howard Chivers. Howard and I were co-captains of the ski team."

Today the Chivers name lives on: Just south of the crest of the pass is Chivers' Ridge, a long, perfectly pitched run dropping down to Trail Creek.

John Litchfield, long retired and now living in Denver, remembers that the skiers did

Dick Durrance

little or no gate training while they were in Jackson. "In those days nobody groomed racecourses—you walked up and raced on what was there. We freeskied on Teton Pass to develop our legs and become accustomed to the Western powder. We were all impressed with the snow. It was Valhalla."

On the day after Christmas, two hundred townspeople gathered atop the pass to watch Durrance and his teammates ski with fixed-heel bindings and short ski poles, revolutionary equipment they'd brought from Europe. It was also the first time Jacksonites saw skiers attack the fall line, a technique Durrance developed while growing up in Germany. He called his trademark turn the "dipsy doodle."

"It's a fall-line turn," Durrance explains. "You're in a slight snowplow, and you dance from one ski to the other, bang-bang-bang-bang. It's a screwy name, but that's what we called it."

"We had a hell of a good time," Litchfield says. "I remember the entrance to the Teton Pass Ranch, where we stayed, had a huge arch of antlers. And I remember that Fred Brown's father wore six-shooters. You can imagine what our group of Easterners thought about that."

And how did the team eventually fare against the University of Washington? "We swamped 'em. We beat the hell out of them," says Litchfield.

Neil Rafferty, who built Snow King's first chairlift, also operated the Ski Jitney, which carried skiers from Jackson to the top of Teton Pass on weekends and holidays.

from Hoback Canyon who performed ski tricks in western clothes and cowboy hats. As a grand finale during an exhibition on Snow King, they jumped through a fiery hoop. "But youngster Bill Saunders stole the show," wrote Gene Downer in the 1973–74 *Teton Annual*, "by sweeping down the mountain and through the flaming hoop right behind the men."

Skiing in Jackson took its greatest leap in 1939, when Neil Rafferty built a rope tow on Snow King. Featuring an idiosyncratic system of detachable handles, the tow is well remembered by Virginia Huidekoper, one of America's top female racers in the late 1930s and early 1940s.

"[The handle] was a pipe with a piece of angle iron on the end, notched, so when your weight went back it would grab the rope," recalls Huidekoper who, at seventy-nine, has the lined face and bright eyes of somebody who has willingly and happily spent all of her life outdoors. "And there was a little rope and board that went around behind," she continues. "You had to ski back down with this piece of pipe and board and rope wrapped around you. OSHA [the Occupational Safety and Health Administration] would have had a fit if they'd seen that setup."

Huidekoper, who still runs her ranch

Above: the Joe Pfeiffer homestead, which stood on Antelope Flats, in Grand Teton National Park, until it was consumed by fire in 1994. Below: Virginia Huidekoper, ski racer, rancher, and founder of the *Jackson Hole News.*

just below Teton Pass, moved permanently to Jackson from Salt Lake City in 1943. A few years later, she, her husband, Jim, and several other avid skiers formed the Jackson Hole Wintersports Association. They raised fifteen thousand dollars, purchased an old ore tramway from Salida, Colorado, and erected it on Snow King. Actual lift-served skiing became a reality in western Wyoming, serving 8,500 skiers in the first season.

"[Snow King] was really a success because it was right there," says Huidekoper. "My kids were brought up on that mountain. Everybody's kids were. You could leave the babies in the bassinet in the station wagon at the bottom of the hill, take a run, then go check on

Below: The moon about to set behind Green River Canyon. The Hobacks, part of Jackson Hole Mountain Resort, are in the foreground.
Right: Because of soaring real estate prices and property taxes, ranching is a fading industry in Jackson Hole.

them. Billy Saunders built a ski shop and a coffee shop at the corner and that was the center, until we built the ski shelter. We got a set of house logs and put it up, just a bunch of volunteers hammering away. It wasn't very complicated."

During the Great Depression and World War II, skiing wove itself inexorably into Jackson Hole's winter life. Early each season before Snow King opened, Neil Rafferty operated a rope tow on Teton Pass, powered by a 1941 army weapons carrier truck. He charged ten cents per ride. Rafferty also ran the ski jitney, a flatbed jeep that provided rides up the old pass road on weekends and holidays.

Farther north, rangers were using skis to explore newly

established Grand Teton National Park. Accompanying the rangers on their tours was a local teenager named Fred Brown, who went on to become a ski racer, ski instructor, mountain guide, geologist, and the first president of the Jackson Ski Club. The true father of backcountry skiing in Jackson Hole, Brown toured extensively across the Tetons in the 1930s and 1940s from his family's dude ranch at the foot of Teton Pass.

One of Brown's frequent ski partners was Paul Petzoldt, who made one of the first

ascents of the Grand Teton (he did it in 1924, as a sixteen-year-old, in cowboy boots), founder of the Tetons' first climbing school, and legendary raconteur and storyteller. Petzoldt recalled that Brown dreamt of establishing a ski area on his property, but "the terrain and the snow and all the other considerations did not make Fred's ranch a practical headquarters for a ski area."

The new lifts installed on Snow King in the late 1930s and 1940s put a further damper on Brown's competing plans. Still, he and Petzoldt

continued to explore the Tetons, wondering if they might find a setting for a ski resort to truly capitalize on the range's colossal terrain. On the west side, they skied Fred's Mountain, where Grand Targhee ski resort sprawls today. Even more promising, however, was a certain mountain on the east side of the range.

"Below Buck Mountain, north of Wilson, there was one mountain that stood out," wrote Petzoldt in his autobiography, *Teton Tales*. "It was clearly visible from my ranch on Ditch Creek [across the valley] and it was obvious it had great potential for skiing."

Petzoldt was referring, of course, to Rendezvous Mountain, where Jackson Hole Mountain Resort sits today. With his brother

Curly and Fred Brown, Petzoldt skied Rendezvous several times in the mid-1930s.

"We did go up there on three or four different occasions," recalled Petzoldt in a 1996 interview with Jackson writer Tom Turiano. "Once I went up there alone, taking all day to climb up three or four thousand feet. I went completely to the top on two or three occasions . . . and spent a long time skiing down the mountain. But it was difficult, and we knew it would be difficult for beginners unless there were places lower on the mountain that would be level enough to teach skiing."

However promising the terrain, Petzoldt claimed he and Brown didn't have the resources to build a ski resort. "These were dreams, impos-

sible dreams," he said. "We had no money, and we had no connections. We just knew that some day there was going to be a big ski area there. If a ski area was ever really developed, that's where it would be."

Petzoldt may have been merely prophetic. Or, if you believe *Teton Tales*, which utterly contradicts his "impossible dreams" recollection, he acted on his prescience, becoming the first investor in the property that today is Teton Village. He wrote that after

World War II, he did have "a little money" and bought the Crystal Springs Ranch for seventeen thousand dollars. But before the sale was out of escrow, "the man who sold me the ranch came with tears in his eyes saying his wife was going to divorce him if he went through with the sale." Petzoldt sold it back, but not without extracting a tidy two-thousand-dollar profit on the resale.

Petzoldt, who died in 1999, was famed for his tall tales, and this may have been one of them. After all, there's no trace of Petzoldt's name in the Teton County land records. But Petzoldt and Fred Brown certainly had the drive, stamina, and skill to make the first ski descent from Rendezvous Mountain. And any imaginative skier, during such a descent, would have been able to envision Rendezvous's steep flanks as a world-class ski area.

But Petzoldt, whatever his premonitions, didn't forge ahead with his ideas. Nor did any other locals suggest a ski resort be built in the Tetons. It took two newcomers, arriving with fresh eyes and grand ambitions, to notice what the locals did not: Just a few miles north of Teton Pass lay a mountain that would wholly redefine the locals' favorite winter sport.

chapter 3

THE MAKING OF A MOUNTAIN

It's a common observation, and a matter of local pride, that Jackson Hole Mountain Resort doesn't look like a "mountain resort." Missing are the hallmarks of a typical American ski area—the wide, artificial swaths of snow streaming down a forested hill-side like the fingers of an albino god. Instead, Jackson Hole's trails blend seamlessly with the avalanche paths and scree fields that abound in the Tetons. Indeed, slide paths and scree fields are the basis for many of the resort's runs.

Looking up at the Hobacks, Laramie Bowl, and the Moran Faces from the Teton Village parking lot, it seems only natural that somebody would have come along and draped lifts across those airy ridges, bowls, and crags. The place practically begs to be skied. (Local climbing guide and diehard backcountry skier Wesley Bunch likes to chide, "They ruined a perfectly good ski area when they put those lifts in.")

But Rendezvous Mountain, however ideal for development, was not easily tamed. Though it's hard to imagine the southern Tetons without the ski area's aerial tram, the famous cableway almost self-destructed, both financially and literally, before it was finished. Even more remarkably, the initial ski resort developers ignored the Tetons altogether, intending to locate the region's first major ski area in an entirely different range.

In the late 1950s, though many Jackson locals thought their mountains well-suited to a destination ski resort, no one came forward to build one. The ball only got rolling when a group of Salt Lake City investors arrived, bearing plans for a large-scale resort in the Gros Ventre Range, across the valley from the Tetons. Their chosen location was upper Cache Creek, a deep canyon that funnels directly into the town of Jackson. Excited by the prospect of steady wintertime tourist traffic, a group of local businessmen hauled a mobile home up the canyon to serve as a base of operations.

But at least one local was unimpressed with the prospective setting. "The terrain was either steeper than a cow's face or flat," said Paul McCollister to the *Jackson Hole News* in 1976. "There was no in between to speak of."

Born in Columbus, Ohio, reared in Southern California and educated at Stanford University, Paul Wayne McCollister had retired to Jackson Hole in 1956. Eternally optimistic, fast talking, and boundlessly energetic, he was a born salesman.

Peak 10,450, or Rendezvous Mountain in the early 1960s, mostly untouched by man.

Left: Jackson Hole Ski Resort founders Paul McCollister and Alex Morley, before construction of the resort. Above: Morley works the phones. Below: Willy Schaeffler, University of Denver ski coach and ski-area expert, uses a hand level to lay out ski trails. Right: Rendezvous Mountain above an embryonic Teton Village.

He began his career at his family's radio advertising firm, then became part owner of the *San Jose Shopping News*. Having fallen for the Tetons on a 1942 hunting trip, McCollister bought a home on a Grand Teton National Park inholding in 1950 and retired to Wyoming six years later. Though he planned to assume the role of a gentleman hunter, fisherman, and skier, friends knew he'd soon be bored. ("At least buy a gas station," suggested a California business associate, "and go down once a week and count the tires.")

Instead, McCollister bought a small cattle operation at the base of the Tetons and became a ski racing aficionado, traveling to the Winter Olympics in Cortina d'Ampezzo, Italy, in 1956 and spending a month skiing around Europe. When he returned to Wyoming, the Salt Lake investors, seeking partners, presented their plans to him at his home on Antelope Flats.

"I was the president of the Jackson Hole Ski Club," McCollister said to the *News*, "and they also thought I might have four or five dollars in the bank."

The Salt Lake group also approached Wyoming son Alex Morley, who'd grown up ski racing, served as an Air Force pilot during World War II, and subsequently fashioned a successful building and real estate development

company in his native Cheyenne. By the late 1950s, Morley was looking for a new challenge and a new home. Having moored a sailboat on Jackson Lake for years, he, too, decided to move to Jackson Hole and bought a home on a Grand Teton National Park inholding not far from McCollister's.

"These people in Salt Lake had given me Paul's name," recalls Morley, interviewed by phone from his present home in Bend, Oregon. "I contacted him because we

were going to be neighbors up there. We started talking about this project up Cache Creek and both [of us] decided it wasn't very good."

For a third opinion, McCollister turned to Willy Schaeffler, University of Denver ski coach, whom he'd met at the 1960 Olympics at Squaw Valley. An acknowledged ski-area expert, Schaeffler accepted McCollister's invitation to look at the Cache Creek location and was duly unimpressed by the mellow terrain. (According to Vail founder Pete Seibert, Schaeffler thought likewise about Vail's gentle slopes.)

But the prospect of developing a ski resort had fired McCollister's imagination. He began surveying the Tetons from the air in pursuit of an ideal venue, and like Paul Petzoldt, was struck by

Rendezvous Mountain's breadth and consistent pitch. Convinced he'd found his mountain, McCollister hired Schaeffler to begin a snow feasibility study on Rendezvous. He also sold his interest in the Cache Creek project, rankling local business owners who wanted to keep a destination ski resort closer to town. McCollister, however, was less interested in local relations than a global reputation. After spending another winter in the Alps in 1961, he returned to Wyoming determined to build a resort in the Tetons to rival those at Davos, Kitzbühel, St. Moritz, and Zermatt. In search of a partner, he turned to his neighbor, Morley, who himself had been gazing across his front yard and imagining a ski resort within the mighty range that defined the western horizon. Morley was particularly

taken with Buck Mountain, the sprawling southern monarch of Grand Teton National Park. McCollister convinced Morley that developing Buck would be problematic and that Rendezvous, just south of the park, would serve as a better ski mountain. Morley acquiesced, and the two joined forces.

So much for early retirement.

In the summer of 1961 and the winter that followed, Morley's and McCollister's idea gathered momentum as they explored

their chosen mountain. McCollister and his son Mike climbed to the summit on horseback, finding a cairn from a previous expedition—perhaps Paul Petzoldt's. Today, their campsite from that trip is marked by the Campground run near the upper terminus of the Bridger Gondola. On Christmas 1962, McCollister, Morley, Dr. John Gramlich, and Ernie Hirsch of the Forest Service climbed partway up, making their first ski turns on the mountain.

"Here's this huge mountain," recalls Morley, "and John Gramlich and I collided in the powder that day."

Later that winter, McCollister and climbing guide Barry Corbet skied from the summit of Rendezvous Mountain and at the winter's end, Willy Schaeffler made his final assessment of the mountain's feasibility.

"The ski terrain which we found over the six-square-mile area is absolutely ideal and overwhelming," he reported. "The structure of this whole mountain convinces me that it is a close-to-ideal setup for a major summer and winter recreation development."

"That squared 100 percent with what I thought," said McCollister to the *News*. He'd already had the foresight, in December 1961, to pay

The valley tram station under construction. The matching structures over the men's heads are curve beams. The track cables, once installed, would run from the mountain's summit, over the curve beams, to the counterweights suspended below the tram station, each of which weighed 104 tons.

$12,600 for an option to purchase the Crystal Springs Ranch from the Clatterbaughs. Making things official, McCollister and Morley formed the Jackson Hole Ski Corporation in 1963, bringing in Gordon Graham, McCollister's former partner in the *San Jose Shopping News*, as a third investor. The final price they paid in September, 1963, for the 166-acre ranch was $255,000, or about $1,355 per acre.

The new custodians of Jackson Hole's long skiing tradition had everything they needed to push skiing into a higher realm: a great mountain, the Tetons' deep snowfall, and a new company. Only one question was left, a question that would haunt the Ski Corporation for the next three decades—how to pay for their grand endeavor.

In the *San Francisco Chronicle*, McCollister found an article on the Area Redevelopment Administration (ARA), a federal government program that loaned funds to depressed communities that relied on seasonal economies. Though some locals were miffed at the suggestion that their placid valley was "depressed," it was true that in the winter, employment in Jackson all but evaporated. McCollister and Morley pounced on the opportunity, hoping to receive $975,000 from

Will Success Spoil Jackson Hole?

BY THE EDITORS OF SKIING MAGAZINE
SKIING, OCTOBER 1965

Tucked away in the northwest corner of Wyoming, just south of Yellowstone and Grand Teton National Parks, is the most impressive new skiing area in the U.S. It's Jackson Hole (as distinguished from Jackson's Hole, the valley in which it is located), and the knowledgeable insist it takes more than pictures or a casual look from the base terminal to understand what the great appeal is. It's got to be skied to be believed.

To be sure, the statistics are most impressive. Jackson has the largest native skiing mountain by a substantial margin—in fact, there are only a handful of areas in Europe that top it. It has an aerial tramway, the second in the U.S. built primarily with skiers in mind, that will hoist impatient skiers the entire 4,135 vertical feet in less than eight minutes. Eventually, it will have 10 lifts and 50 miles of slopes and trails, and a complete mountain village with a dozen or so hotels. In short, it has a whale of a lot of mountain, and a whale of a lot of facilities to go with it.

The big attraction at Jackson Hole will be the giant aerial tramway and the terrain it serves. In a typical descent, averaging between three and four miles of downhill running, the skier can encounter almost every challenge and every conceivable snow condition. Not that there aren't easier and more convenient ways off the 10,466-foot summit, but the point of the tramway—now being rushed to completion by a small army of iron-workers and cable stringers—is to provide "endless variety" in the more literal sense

An early ad in SKIING, expressing more optimism about the completion of the tram than was warranted. Notice the placement of the Grand Teton and Mount Owen.

of the phrase. In the course of his run, a skier will delight in roaring through steep cirques, over mountain meadows and benches, through lightly tree-studded slopes, and down trails with constantly changing pitch. It is the sort of variety only a really big mountain can provide.

There is anxiety among the conservation-minded at the great commercial endeavor coming to the Grand Tetons. Will the coming influx of skiers violate this combination of Alpine beauty and frontier Americana? Succinctly, no. The mountains are too immense, and the development is too well planned. Skiing's gain in this case is not necessarily wildlife's loss. And what a gain it is—we repeat, you have to ski it to believe it.

Above: U.S. Senator and Jackson native Cliff Hansen rides the work tram to the summit of Rendezvous Mountain. Right: The work tram was used to carry materials for the aerial tram to the summit. Far right: Workers prepare to winch the aerial tram's track cables, manufactured in Switzerland by E. Fatzer A.G., to the top of Rendezvous.

the ARA, a substantial chunk of the project's $1.6 million budget.

With prodding from Wyoming governor and Jackson native Cliff Hansen, the state legislature passed a special bill allowing the state to participate in the program. A few days before Christmas 1963, McCollister received the call he'd been waiting for: "Paul, how would you like a million-dollar Christmas present?" asked U.S. Senator Gail McGee.

The partners leapt into action, contracting Lander, Wyoming, architects Bob Corbett and Gene Dehnert to design the base resort and hiring Willy Schaeffler to help lay out the trails.

Morley found the process of mapping out the trails as fatiguing as he did exciting. "We hired a helicopter, and Willy and I would fly up to the

top of the mountain with rolls of flagging tape, then we'd run down the mountain," he recalls. "Boy, he was a tough guy. I could hardly keep up with him. We'd run down tying flags where the ski trails would go, and the helicopter would be waiting for us at the bottom; then we'd go back up. We did that for two or three days in a row, and I was just exhausted at the end of each day. We laid out the whole mountain in that short a time."

To name the mountain's trails and features, McCollister and Morley adopted a simple

system: Bowls bore the names of Wyoming cities (Laramie, Riverton, Sheridan, Casper), and ridges were named for some of the early mountain men (Colter, Sublette, Hoback, Ashley). The mountain itself, officially dubbed Peak 10,450 by the U.S. Geological Survey, was renamed Rendezvous Mountain at the suggestion of Morley's neighbor, artist Conrad Schweiring. As for the resort's lower northern peak, the Ski Corporation's first employee, George Fleming, thought he'd unearthed the perfect name. Hired to bulldoze a road to the ski area's summit, Fleming dug up a huge, ancient bear trap on the subpeak's flanks. He proposed the name Bear Trap Mountain. McCollister would have none of it, choosing the Euro-flavored Après Vous instead.

With his son Bruce's help, Morley used a hand level to lay out the road to Rendezvous's summit. As they zigzagged up the mountain, Fleming followed behind in the Ski Corp's first piece of machinery, a D-8 tractor.

"Bruce was just a high school kid," says Morley. "He and I had the darndest time doing that. The mosquitoes—you'd think the whole mountain was alive from the buzzing noise of the mosquitoes."

Left: In 1965, without a real tram to feature in publicity shots, Jackson Hole photographer Jim Elder resorted to sandwiching a photo of a European tram with the Grand Teton. Right: Upper Rendezvous Mountain, before the aerial tram.

Blood-sucking insects, however, turned out to be the least of the problems. Due to heavy snowfall in May 1964, construction on the aerial tram couldn't start until well into the summer. In fact, at the groundbreaking ceremony on April 2, 1964, Howard Head, founder of the Head Ski Company, dug with a ski and never hit anything but snow. Two days of excavation with dynamite and a bulldozer were required to reach the ground.

Meanwhile the contract for building the tram had been awarded to Willamette Construction Company, from Portland, Oregon, which had put in the lowest bid, at $815,000. Though McCollister accepted the bid, Morley was wary and insisted the company put up a construction bond, a prophetic decision. Faced with a project more ambitious than they'd planned for, Willamette soon went bankrupt. The future of Jackson Hole Mountain Resort hung in the balance until Morley, after making repeated trips to the Portland bond office, was able to collect on the bond and find another contractor.

The new contractor, John Halverson, had scant better luck. The winter of 1964–65 was brutally cold and windy, slowing construction

and multiplying costs. As the track cables were winched to the summit, the winch drum broke, and the weight of the cable pulled the cable dangerously tight against the collapsed machinery.

"If they'd have cut it loose, the cable would have flown to Nebraska, for heaven's sake," recalls Morley. "It was a terrible problem, and this was in the middle of winter. Oh, God, was it tough. But they were a very competent construction company, and they figured out a way to do it—they tied off the cable, anchored it into some

concrete, and gradually released the tension. All of this took time, took days, weeks, a month or more, but they finally got it repaired."

Such delays—the drum would break again before the cable was finally in place—drove the costs skyward. The final tally for construction of the tram was $2.5 million. Though the Ski Corporation had to pay only a third of the final price (the extra cost was borne by the construction and bond companies), the problems had delayed the tram's opening by nearly one and a half years.

But the tram's construction cost even more than time and money. To bring materials up the mountain, Willamette first built a smaller wooden tram, with one car for workers and another for

Below: Resort cofounder Paul McCollister surveys a brand new tram car, tested for the first time in summer 1966.

cement and materials. Only the passenger-carrying side of the tramway was equipped with emergency brakes; workers were warned not to ride on the other side. Nevertheless, one day two workers, Woodrow Linville and Gustav Grabowski, decided to gamble, jumping into the cement bucket for the descent from the summit. A faulty splice in a cable separated, and the bucket screamed down the tramway, killing both men.

A similar fate might have befallen Morley and McCollister had it not been for quick thinking and action. On a particularly cold, windy day, the resort founders could not coax the tram builders to go to the top of the mountain, so they decided to shame the men into

working by heading up the work tram themselves. Nearing the huge cliffs just below the summit, they saw to their horror that the wind had piled snow into a cornice atop the cliffs and that the tram cable was sawing through it. Morley radioed the operator below to stop the tram, but the radio wasn't working. The car hit the cornice, straining to continue. Frantically, Morley shouted into the radio as the cable tightened.

"I expected it to break," remembers Morley, "and [that] Paul and I in the little car

Right: The first two buildings in Teton Village: the Seven Levels Inn (now the Village Center) and the clock tower. Below: Teton Village during the second ski season, 1966–67, included the Seven Levels, the Alpenhof, and the Sojourner Inn.

would plunge down the face of the rocks to the bottom five hundred feet down. I was afraid that if the cable did not break that the whole cornice could collapse and carry the work tram, towers, and cable, over the cliff."

Luckily, the operator, recognizing something was wrong, threw the switch to stop the tram. But with no way to know what was actually happening, he was afraid to reverse the cars. Tying into a rope they'd brought along, Morley scrambled out of the car and over the cornice, where he

dug in to belay McCollister as he climbed out. Then, while McCollister belayed him, Morley shoveled the cornice away, eventually freeing the car. Getting the radio to work again, they reboarded the tram.

"We rode to the bottom," says Morley. "Paul and I told the workers that it was fine up on the mountain—go on up and get to work. And they did."

The tram was finally finished late that summer, carrying the first passengers to the summit of Rendezvous Mountain on July 31, 1966. Jackson Hole ski resort had already had its first winter season, however, having opened for business without the tram on December 26, 1965. In the months before this limited season, the Ski Corporation

The Flagship of Jackson Hole

It has to be one the most exhilarating rides in the United States.

First you squeeze through the turnstile on the tram dock in Teton Village; then you squeeze into the fifty-four-passenger car, painted Cardinal Red in honor of Paul McCollister's alma mater, Stanford University. Swinging away from the tram dock, the car accelerates, beginning its two-and-a-half-mile long journey to the 10,450-foot summit of Rendezvous Mountain. The village rapidly recedes. After rumbling past the first suspension tower, the car travels a remarkable 6,000 linear feet before passing Tower Two. The lower mountain, mottled by firs and aspens and slashed by ski runs, skims past. As the car nears Tower Three, the trees thin and the view of the Teton Range widens to the north. The tram climbs over one high precipice, then another. Tower Four approaches and recedes. The tram sails across Tensleep Bowl, reaching its highest point above ground, about 280 feet. To the north is the vast sweep of the Tetons. To the south is a wall of rock, incised by S'n'S Couloir and Corbet's Couloir. Everything is snow, rock, and sky. Finally, as the tram passes Tower Five and slows, the tram attendant makes his announcement ("Can I have your attention,

open chairlift," explains Morley. "They get too nervous. And we wanted the summer business. We thought that's how we'd make most of our money. That's the main reason we decided on an aerial tramway."

Even before Jackson Hole's tram was fully conceived, word spread of the Ski Corporation's trailblazing intentions. Vancouver-based designer Robert McLellan contacted Jackson Hole as soon as he heard rumors of a tramway to be built in the Tetons. Having designed trams for the U.S. government's Distant Early Warning system in Alaska, he got the job.

The design was ingenious—with each car riding on two track cables instead of the customary one, a smaller, 1 3/4 inch diameter of cable could be used and the slack from the haul cable could be cradled in carriers suspended between the towers. This allowed for the great distance, of more than a mile, between Towers, One and Two. It also made the tram more stable in the face of the Tetons, furious storms.

To save money on the tram's construction, McLellan placed all the drive and tension equipment at the base of the mountain, rather than at the top, as is typical for a "jig-back system" that sends one car up as the other comes down. However well designed, the tram got off to a rocky start. The winch used to haul the cables to the top of the mountain broke twice. The initial contractor went bankrupt. During its construction, two men were killed on the work tram, constructed to move materials up the mountain. (See pp. 53-54) And the tram ended up costing three times as

One of the first two tram cars, manufactured by Traunsteinwerkstatten in Austria.

please? Rendezvous Mountain from the tram is recommended for skiers of expert abilities only . . . ") and you emerge on the Upper Tram dock in an utterly different world from the one you left 10 minutes earlier and 4,139 vertical feet below.

No other lift ride in the continental U.S. compares, either in drama or in continuous vertical gain. And no other lift in this country represents as great a leap in tramway engineering.

When Paul McCollister, Alex Morley, and Gordon Graham founded Jackson Hole Ski Resort, many European ski resorts had trams, but only one other U.S. ski area did—Cannon Mountain in New Hampshire—and that one was fairly short. Jackson Hole's tram, however, was not built as a gimmick or in imitation of Verbier or Kitzbühel. There was simply no more effective way to transport skiers to the top of such a craggy, stormy mountain. An even more important consideration, according to Alex Morley, were summer tourists.

"A lot of tourists who aren't skiers are afraid to sit on an

much as initially expected and taking almost twice as long to build. The frustration continued after the tram opened—its motors, which were supposed to last 20 years, burned out, temporarily replaced by portable diesel engines. And another worker was killed when he fell from one of the cars.

It's been smooth sailing since then, aside from a few anxious moments. In 1976, telephone lines shorted out and the tram ground to a sudden halt, derailing half the wheels of one carriage. Ascending 200 feet to the hanging car, patrolmen Dean Moore and Bob Sealander used a canvas bag to lower 22 people to the ground. In 1990, soon after the old cars were replaced, the new, electronically operated doors opened mid-ride, requiring another evacuation. And in February, 1996, the tram's brakes suddenly and inexplicably engaged. It was five hours before all passengers could be lowered the 200 feet to the ground, but nobody was hurt. In fact, no public passenger has ever been injured on the tram, though the tram has carried millions of people to the summit of Rendezvous Mountain. And though the tram was built almost four decades ago, it will probably carry many more millions high into the Tetons.

U.S. Senator Gail McGee, instrumental in securing the government loan for the construction of Jackson Hole Ski Resort, speaks to the crowd during groundbreaking ceremonies, such as they were, on April 2, 1964. Behind him are cofounders Alex Morley and Paul McCollister.

had scrambled to finish Lifts 1, 2, and 3 (now known as Eagle's Rest, Teewinot, and Après Vous). Unfortunately, to add insult to injury, Jackson Hole's first customers didn't have much snow to ski on, as the winter got off to a late start. The final tally for that first season was a mere nineteen thousand skier days.

It was a humble beginning for such an imposing place. Nevertheless, McCollister and Morley deserve credit for a staggering achievement, given their modest starting capital, the chal-

lenging topography, the brutal weather, and the builders' travails. Without their tenacity, the ski resort might have failed before any tram tower adorned Rendezvous's silhouette.

"Building that ski area," says Morley, "I had the greatest time I ever had in my entire life."

Running the ski area, however, turned out to be far more onerous. The very ruggedness that had attracted Morley and McCollister to the Tetons in the first place proved a hurdle. The mountain was steep, remote, and cold. Convincing skiers that these were actually positive attributes would require reserves of pluck and determination that the construction of the ski resort had only begun to tap. ❋

chapter 4

THE MCCOLLISTER ERA: 1965 TO 1992

TRUE GRIT

Nearly two centuries after they passed through Jackson Hole, mountain men Jedediah Smith, Jim Bridger, and Davey Jackson are still glorified. Historians retrace and debate their routes through the Northern Rockies. Wilderness areas, national forests, and towns are named after them. Museums have been devoted to their rifles and to the rocks they inscribed in passing. Though none settled permanently in this area, the trappers are the reigning mythic figures of Jackson Hole.

Yet men who passed through more recently or who still live here have made far more indelible marks on the mountains that define this valley. Whereas Jackson and Bridger considered the peaks merely a place to lay their traps, these modern heroes developed and acted on passions for the mountains as fierce as the Tetons themselves. There was John D. Rockefeller, Jr., who secretly used his fortune to prevent the debasement of the Tetons' foothills. There was William Owen, the first to summit the Grand Teton in 1898. There were Fritiof Fryxell, Paul Petzoldt, and Glenn Exum, who spent their lives studying, exploring, and guiding throughout the range. And there was Bill Briggs, who, alone and with his right leg fused at the hip, made the first ski descent from the top of the Grand in 1971.

The list would be incomplete without Paul McCollister, the advertising salesman from California who retired to Jackson Hole, then spent the rest of his life pursuing a vision of a ski resort in the Tetons that would rival anything in the Alps.

It was not just McCollister's vision in the beginning; his partners, Alex Morley and Gordon Graham, were just as captivated by the idea of founding the greatest ski resort in North America. But Graham soon backed out, deciding instead to enter Jackson's burgeoning real estate industry. So did Morley, five years later, when it became clear that McCollister's business strategies diverged sharply from his own.

McCollister was not a man given to compromise. Or pessimism. Or strict obedience to a balance sheet's bottom line. He was a master salesman who'd polished his Jackson Hole sales pitch to a fine sheen. Convinced of the infallibility of his ideals, he refused to relinquish them until they finally dissolved in his hands.

But in 1965, it was unimaginable that McCollister would ever be disassociated from the Jackson Hole ski resort. After all, he, Morley, and Graham had achieved the unthinkable, opening the United States' most ambitious ski resort in one of the nation's

Three constants during the late-1980s and 1990s: Doug Coombs, Corbet's Couloir, and a crowd.

Left: Pepi Stiegler signs his contract as Paul McCollister looks on. Above: Buddy Werner, who would have been Jackson Hole's ski school director had he not been killed in an avalanche in St. Moritz in 1964.

most remote spots. They'd even convinced the government to lend them nearly a million dollars to do it. Granted, the resort's tram was still under construction, but work was progressing and the builders had managed to erect three lifts in time for the December 26, 1965, opening.

Even more impressive was Teton Village. With its sharply steepled clock tower and tight cluster of hotels—the Alpenhof, Sojourner Inn, and Seven Levels Inn—it truly resembled the Tyrolean-style village McCollister and Morley had envisioned.

Moreover, the founders had hired a hero named Pepi Stiegler— a square-jawed, blue-eyed, Olympic gold medalist—to lead their ski instructors and bolster the resort's image as a place where world cham-

pions came to ski. From the beginning McCollister, a devoted racing fan, had wanted a famous athlete to direct the Jackson Hole ski school. His first choice, however, was not a European, but Wallace "Buddy" Werner, the best American ski racer of the 1950s and early 1960s. A native of Steamboat Springs, Colorado, a member of three Olympic teams, and winner of the prestigious Hahnenkamm downhill in Kitzbühel, Austria, Werner was a natural choice to run the ski school. Even

Pepi Stiegler
FROM AUSTRIAN HERO TO WYOMING COWBOY

Born in Lienz, Austria, in 1937, Josef "Pepi" Stiegler learned to ski by age five, began racing at thirteen, and won the Austrian junior championship only two years later. At twenty-one, he gained a spot on the national team. His first Olympic medal came at the 1960 Winter Games at Squaw Valley, where he won silver in the giant slalom. Though this could hardly be considered a poor showing, Stiegler was unsatisfied, particularly by his fifth-place finish in slalom.

"I decided right there in Squaw Valley to specialize in technical events," Stiegler says. "Specializing wasn't done, generally. But looking back, it was a good decision."

Indeed, 1961 was the high point of Stiegler's career as a slalom specialist. He won the Austrian national championship and three international slalom races. And at the 1964 Winter Olympics in Innsbruck, Austria, he captured his gold medal in slalom and took bronze in the giant slalom. He was cheered as a national hero and subsequently named coach of the Austrian national team. But his tenure didn't last long. After only a year and a half, he developed a distaste for racing's bureaucracy.

"At first it sounded prestigious to be the coach of a national team," he recalls, "but when spring came around, I started observing how it all functioned with the sponsors and manufacturers, and I thought, 'I don't like this.' At that very moment, when I felt most strongly that I didn't want to do this the rest of my life, the phone rang. It was Paul [McCollister]."

Stiegler went on to direct the Jackson Hole Ski School for twenty-nine

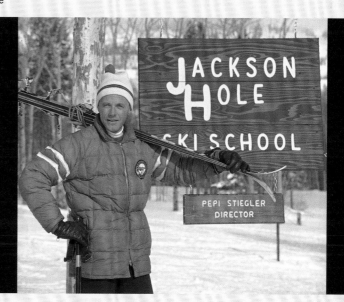

Pepi Stiegler in his first year as ski school director.

years. In 1994, he became the resort's director of skiing, a title he still holds today. Though Stiegler's passions have widened in scope—he'll soon complete a bachelor's degree in English literature at Montana State University, finishing an education he put on hold while racing for the Austrian ski team—he's still a devoted skier and coach. In fact, his two children, Sepi and Resi, are competitive racers, and Pepi still leads a ski camp at Jackson Hole each December. He also leads daily tours of the resort, free of charge, from the top terminal of the Bridger Gondola.

Watching Stiegler lead guests down Amphitheater Run, one can't help but notice that the efficient, powerful form that earned him gold, silver, and bronze Olympic medals hasn't faded.

"He's so bloody smooth," says Johannes Albrecht, a University of Illinois architecture professor who joined a "Ski with Pepi" tour in March 2001. "And he skis so unassumingly. There's no fuss about it. It looks so casual. Only when you ski behind him do you get the idea of how fast he could ski in the bumps and still make it appear as if he's looking at the scenery."

Left: Pepi Stiegler skis to glory on the slalom course at the 1964 Olympics at Innsbruck.
Above: Billy Kidd, Pepi Stiegler, and Jimmie Heuga on the podium at the Innsbruck Olympics.

Stiegler concedes that. "Buddy Werner would have been perfect for Paul," he says now.

But on April 12, 1964, Werner was killed in an avalanche outside St. Moritz, Switzerland, while skiing for filmmaker Willy Bogner's cameras. To honor Werner, McCollister named the race course on Après Vous after him, and then resumed his search for a ski school director.

His next choice was Austrian Othmar Schneider, the 1952 Olympic slalom champion. But Schneider, already ski school director at Michigan's Boyne Mountain, turned him down. McCollister asked him for a recommendation, and Schneider suggested Pepi Stiegler, whom he had coached at the Squaw Valley games. While in Europe,

McCollister made his well-timed phone call to Stiegler, and at their subsequent meeting in Innsbruck, McCollister used his every power of persuasion on the young Austrian.

"Man, did he do a sales job on me," remembers Stiegler. "Unbelievable. He could do a salesman job on Jackson Hole that was unreal. I don't know what you'd have to do to say no."

Stiegler, however, wasn't quite ready to say yes. McCollister tried again while Stiegler

was coaching in South America. It was the summer of 1965, and the Jackson Hole resort would open in a few months. Though he'd already hired a half-dozen instructors from Europe, McCollister still lacked a ski school director, so he flew in Stiegler from Chile for a visit.

"I was very, very impressed, to say the least," Stiegler says with a laugh. "He took me to the top of Rendezvous in a helicopter; his son Mike drove me up to Yellowstone to look at all the bears running around on the highway. I told

Paul the only thing standing in the way was the contract with the Austrian team and he said that's not going to be a problem. I accepted the offer and came to work on November 1."

He needn't have rushed. The ski area did scant business its first season. Recalls Bill Ashley, founder of Teton Village Sports, which was then located under the Seven Levels Inn, "I didn't have a single customer on opening day. Neither did the Seven Levels."

On December 28, the entire ski school taught three lessons. "That was a hard beginning," says Stiegler, "a really hard beginning."

Compounding problems were the frequent setbacks in the aerial tram's construction and the uncooperative weather. The resort, in fact,

Above: Forest Stearns buys Jackson Hole's first season pass in 1965. Above right: The Après Vous Lift, originally Lift #3, was one of three lifts running in Jackson Hole's first season, 1965–66. Right: Pepi Stiegler with his ski instructors, 1966.

closed in March for lack of snow, having tallied only nineteen thousand skier days in its inaugural season.

McCollister, at least, was determined to get his money's worth from the ski instructors he'd contracted for the whole season and assigned them to various projects around Teton Village. Austrian Herman Schmutzer, for example, was assigned to paint the lift shack at the upper end of Eagle's Rest. Schmutzer was none too pleased.

Walking past the lift shack, McCollister asked, "Well, Herman, how are you doing with the painting?"

Schmutzer snapped back, "I came here as a ski instructor. I did not come from Vienna to paint plywood."

Laughing, McCollister dubbed the proud Austrian "Rembrandt."

Schumtzer, not surprisingly, did not come back to Jackson Hole for a second season. But McCollister, Morley, and Stiegler forged ahead, trying desperately to sell little-known Jackson Hole ski resort to the world at large. In McCollister's mind, the answer lay in ski racing. Even before the resort opened, he'd offered to host the final Fédération Internationale de Ski (FIS) races of the 1967

Above: The town of Wilson hosted a rodeo for visitors and competitors during the first Wild West Classic, in March, 1967. Right: Cowboy hats were given away at the Wild West Classic. Far right: Jean Claude Killy clowns around during the awards ceremony.

season—the first FIS season, incidentally, to include American venues.

Sponsored by the resort and orchestrated by the Jackson Hole Ski Club, the Wild West Classic (as the FIS race was called) was held in March and embraced every opportunity to show off the Wyoming setting. A rodeo was held in Wilson (several ski racers tried to compete, to their coaches' alarm), and at the awards banquet at the Cowboy Bar, race winners were given silver spurs.

On the snow, Canadian Nancy Greene swept all three races and came from behind in a stirring upset to snatch the World Cup title from France's Marielle Goitschel and Annie Famose. As for the men, Frenchman Jean-Claude Killy had already clinched the World Cup title, having won twenty-three races that season. Though he won just one of the three races at the Wild West Classic, he was buoyed enough by his overall title and the surprisingly good skiing at Jackson Hole to declare to *Sports Illustrated*, "If there is a better ski mountain in the U.S., I haven't skied it."

McCollister was ebullient. Within a week he announced his intention to host the 1970 FIS World Championships. That summer he and Alex Morley traveled to Beirut, Lebanon, for the FIS International Congress, where the

Below: Not all the gates on Jackson Hole's Nastar course are stationary.
Right: Sparse crowds meant many peaceful moments in the resort's first few years.

venue for the 1970 Worlds would be decided. They brought with them fifty cowboy hats to give to delegates. The gifts were popular—Morley remembers seeing cowboy hats all over Beirut, bobbing ahead of him in the crowded streets—but Jackson Hole lost the World Championships to Val Gardena, Italy.

It was a dispiriting defeat for McCollister, who thought it vital that "a major destination resort held world-class races every year," as he told *Jackson Hole Magazine* in 1992. But as Morley saw it, races did not translate into receipts. "I told Paul we've got to change the way we're running this place," he recalls. "Stop trying to get the Olympics and the FIS Championships, devote more of our time to attracting people who are going to ski and buy lift tickets, get more hotels built here, and Paul said, 'Nope,

we've got to keep going with the racing because that's what's glamorous.' But that doesn't put dollars in your pockets."

And their pockets were chronically empty, much to Morley's chagrin. "After we started operating, we didn't get the numbers of skiers we'd hoped to," he says. "I'd be scraping the bottom of the barrel trying to pay the ski patrolmen and the instructors and the light bill. Boy, it got tough."

Sometimes it got desperate. To raise cash, Morley and McCollister held "fire sales" of

the real estate surrounding Teton Village, offering half-acre home lots for ten or fifteen thousand dollars, lifetime ski passes included. They also sold their inholdings in Grand Teton National Park to the park service, sinking the funds into the ski resort instead. After founding the Jackson Hole Golf and Country Club (now Jackson Hole Golf and Tennis) near the airport, the pair sold that, too, in order to shore up the ski corporation's finances. Repeatedly, they borrowed money from banks in Casper or from friends with deeper pockets.

Says Morley, "I got hold of King Curtis [a physician in the Seattle area], whom I used to go cross-country skiing with, and I asked him if he didn't want to become part-owner in the ski corporation, and he did. Well, he saved our bacon a couple or three times by injecting one-hundred or two-hundred thousand dollars into the corporation to make our payroll. I tell you, we'd have folded up if I hadn't been able to get that money from him."

Finally, in 1972, Morley bowed out. Having personally guaranteed the government loans that allowed construction of the resort, he could no longer handle the stress of flirting with bankruptcy and sold out to McCollister. "My wife told me if I hadn't made that decision, I'd have been dead in a couple of years," he says.

Left: Harry Baxter, Jackson Hole's marketing director, then vice president of public relations, between 1974 and 1995. Above: A magazine ad from the late-1970s, featuring the "Ski the Big One" promotion.

Morley suspected the resort itself would not last more than a couple of years. But McCollister endured, recruiting Pepi Stiegler to accompany him to ski shows across the country in order to drum up interest in the new resort. It was a hard sell. Though many skiers had heard about Jackson Hole, they'd also heard that the Wyoming resort was too remote, too steep, and too cold. "Everybody told you this," Stiegler recalls. "It was discouraging."

Just as discouraging were his occasional trips to Vail. The Colorado resort had grown quickly while the Wyoming resort struggled. "I'd go to Vail for a master's event or a spring clinic," remembers Stiegler, "and I'd see all their success, and I'd think, 'What the hell are we doing?'"

In 1974, McCollister hired Harry Baxter, former general manager at Sugarloaf Mountain Corporation in Maine, to take over as Jackson Hole's marketing director. A former national whitewater-paddling champion, Baxter leapt wholeheartedly into the murky waters of marketing the resort. One of his first accomplishments, according to Baxter, was landing a contract with Frontier Airlines to charter jets into Jackson Hole, a vital step in addressing the perception that Jackson Hole was "not the most

Each spring for nearly thirty years, a wide swath of meticulously braided tracks would appear on Cody Bowl, the vast slope below Cody Peak's upper pyramid. These were the remnants of Jackson Hole's Powder 8 competition, which for one day every year turned the resort's backcountry into both an athletic venue and an artist's palette.

The very idea of a figure-eight competition was born at Jackson Hole. In 1968, Gene Downer, who worked in marketing for Head Skis, planned a ski competition for ski patrollers from several different resorts. But that winter, the patrol crew at Aspen unionized. In response, Aspen's chairman vowed to fire all the patrollers and replace them if they traveled to Vail for the competition, so it was cancelled.

Resigning from Head soon afterwards, Downer moved to Jackson to found *Teton Magazine*. A ski patrol competition, he reasoned, would bring valuable publicity to his new venture. Artist Terry King suggested instead that Downer host a figure-eight contest, and patroller Denny Ashe suggested he hold it on Cody Bowl.

The competitors would ski in teams of two, crisscrossing each other's tracks and thus form figure eights in the snow. According to the rules, skiers would be judged on "overall track appearance, skier's form, uniformity of distance between skiers during the run, and numbers of turns made during the run." Skiers were also required "to alternate between five large and five small turns during the run."

The competition could not have begun more auspiciously. On the morning of *Teton Magazine*'s inaugural Figure Eight Competition, the March sky was flawlessly blue and sixteen inches of fresh snow filled the bowl. Taking first place among the eleven teams was Pepi Stiegler and Peter Habeler, one of Pepi's instructors, who would go on to make the first ascent of Mount Everest without supplemental oxygen.

Downer didn't let his marketing background go to waste. After the competition, he mailed photos of competitors making tracks below Cody's craggy visage to the Associated Press and United Press International.

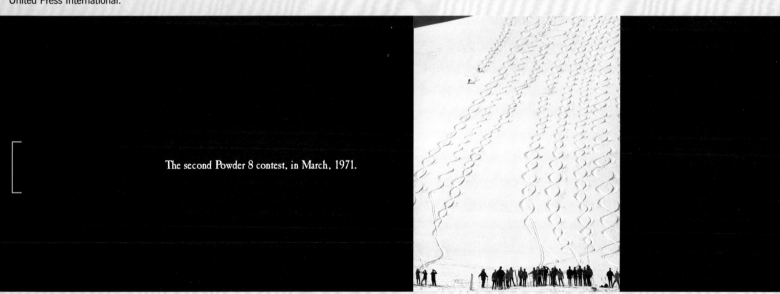

The second Powder 8 contest, in March, 1971.

"It was in March, in late spring, so they ran the pictures everywhere," says Downer, who now owns the Teton Bookstore near Jackson's town square. "It was a good way to kiss winter goodbye. It made the front page of the Munich *Evening Times,* and it ran all over this country. It was amazing, incredible publicity for Jackson Hole ski resort. [But] I don't think [*Teton Magazine*] got a single mention."

The next year, Downer held the competition again at Cody Bowl, then moved it to Edelweiss Bowl, near Teton Pass. Finally, he gave it up. "It was a lot of fun," he says, "but boy, it sure was a lot of work."

Revived in 1975, moved back to Cody Bowl, and renamed first the Grand National Powder 8s and then the U.S. National Powder 8s, the competition was a fixture of Jackson Hole's spring schedule for another twenty-six years. But the novelty of skiing powder in the backcountry was lost when the resort opened its out-of-bounds permanently in 1999, and the very idea of synchronized skiing gradually lost its allure. In the spring of 2001, Franz Fuchsberger and Eric Archer, both of Vail, Colorado, won Jackson Hole's final U.S. National Powder 8s Championship. It was the last time an entire Teton mountainside was transformed into art by skiing's competitive spirit.

Right: A young participant in a Jackson Hole summer race camp, which Pepi Stiegler ran throughout the 1970s on Cody Bowl. Below: Wine, skis, and stretchy sweaters—everything necessary for a mid-1970s Rendezvous Mountain rendezvous.

accessible resort in the country," as *Skiing Magazine* put it in 1970.

"Before then, the only jets to come in here were the Rockefellers' or Air Force One," says Baxter, referring to the trip President John F. Kennedy made to Jackson in the summer of 1963, a few months before he was assassinated. At first, the charter program lost money, but Baxter gradually expanded it, organizing flights from several American cities.

Just as crucial was battling the perception that Jackson Hole was solely an expert's mountain. For this reason, Baxter frowned upon the racing events that McCollister wanted so badly. "All it did was dramatize our expert image," he says. Instead, he tried, somewhat disingenuously, to

market Jackson Hole as "the Gentle Giant," including on trail maps the dubious statement that "there is more intermediate skiing on the small mountain, Après Vous, than 90% of America's best."

Baxter also tried to confront Jackson's frigid image. "I used to do the ski reports," he says. "If it was really cold, I'd somehow forget to give the temperature," he says with a laugh.

He was just as creative as he was crafty, adapting and inventing media-friendly events that continue to this day. In 1975, he revived the

Left: Dick Durrance III. Below: The grand prize in the Ski the Big One promotion—a gold belt buckle, given to those who've amassed one million vertical feet. For some participants, this is just the beginning. Art Burrows of Oakville, Ontario, has amassed more than ten million vertical feet.

Figure Eight Competition, calling it the Powder 8s, as an excuse to host ski and travel writers and in the same year founded the Pole Pedal Paddle race to show off Jackson Hole's variety of springtime sports. But Baxter's signature event was Ski the Big One, which rewarded diligent skiers with bronze, silver, and gold belt buckles, depending on how many vertical feet of skiing they'd logged during successive ski vacations.

"I stole the idea from heli-ski operations, who guarantee so much vertical feet to their

The Untamable Hobacks

In 1811, after a particularly brutal winter in the Northern Rockies, trapper John Hoback and two companions struggled through Jackson Hole on their way back to St. Louis. Laden with beaver pelts, Hoback surely must have cursed the deep snows as he plodded over Teton Pass. How ironic, then, that today his name is affixed to three long, broad ridges renowned for their wintertime blankets of deep, idyllic powder.

Fanning across the southern half of Jackson Hole Mountain Resort and dropping nearly three thousand feet, the South, Middle, and North Hobacks are a hidden Eden, a white nirvana. From Rendezvous Trail, one veers right onto a cattrack and whips down a gladed corridor to a little rise, almost a gate. Break over the rise and the world opens below. Sparsely treed, the three broad ridges are ideally pitched for fast, greedy, GS turns. The Hobacks are meant to be devoured, one's feast made visual by long fans of snow sprayed across the sky.

Locals wait anxiously for the day the ski patrol opens the Hobacks for the season, and they vie to be there first.

The Hobacks

Late in winter, heading to the Hobacks is a gamble; once atop the three ridges, there's no turning back, and one might find anything from corn to miraculously preserved powder to corrugated coral reef. It's wilderness skiing within the resort's boundaries.

If Paul McCollister had had his wish, however, the Hobacks would have been tamed. Hoping to transform them into intermediate-level slopes, he repeatedly asked George Fleming, director of resort operations, to groom the Hobacks. Today this would be considered heresy. Back then it was merely considered foolhardy.

"We kept telling Paul the Hobacks were too steep," recalls Fleming. "But he was always after me to go down them. One day, Dick Randolph, the tram supervisor, called me. We had some new snowcats … and he said, 'I found a way we could get down the Hobacks. I'll meet you at Bear Flat and lead you down.' I agreed, but I didn't feel too good about it. I got there and he said, 'I got the route all picked out. Just follow me.'

"Well, the farther we went, the steeper it got. Pretty soon Dick was veering off to the north, but I couldn't maintain control. I shifted to a higher gear so I could accelerate and turn, but it wasn't happening. I took the fastest ride down the Hobacks anybody ever took. I couldn't even see anything, the snow was coming over the top of the cab. Ski patrol said later, looking at my tracks, I must have been airborne thirty, forty feet at a time.

"I got down to the bottom at Union Pass, where it was level, and finally stopped. There was this guy down there cutting brush. He said, 'My God, I've never seen anything like that in my life.' I said, 'You ought to have been in this thing.' I went in the shop after that and ran into Alex Morley. He said, 'I hear you took a wild ride.' I said, 'I did. I just wished Paul McCollister had been in there with me.'"

Above: Inversions—when still, cold air sinks into the valley—make for frigid temperatures in the town of Jackson and in Teton Village and balmy ones up on the mountain. Left: Where the fun begins: Skiers in the late 1960s disembark the aerial tram at the summit of Rendezvous Mountain.

customers. But why go to the Bugaboos when you could ski one hundred fifty thousand vertical feet right here? That's how I came up with the idea. As soon as somebody got a million vertical feet, I'd take a picture of them in front of the clock tower and get a quote, then send both to their hometown newspaper. It was free publicity. And, of course, that gold belt buckle was a traveling billboard wherever they went. It was a good way to get return business, though I'm sure it probably spoiled a lot of family vacations."

Not the Nebels'. Two of the most enthusiastic participants in Ski the Big One, now called the Vertical Foot Club, were Dot and Charlie Nebel from Denville, New Jersey, who didn't let anything as trifling as age stand between them and their gold belt buckles. Charlie accumulated the footage for his own in only eleven weeks, over a two-year period, when he was eighty-two. And Dot received her million-foot prize when she was eighty-eight.

While racking up thousands of vertical feet might have been a novelty to out-of-towners, for locals, it was a fact of life. With only a few hundred ski bums in Jackson in the late 1960s and early 1970s— and precious few paying guests—the slopes and the lifts

were generally empty. As former patroller Charlie Sands remembers, "You'd ride the tram after Christmas holidays, and there'd be four people on it, and three of them would be patrollers."

Taking full advantage of the empty trams was Alex Morley's son Bruce. In 1969, the younger Morley, Dean Anderson, and ski instructor and former racer Ferdl Fettig broke the world record for vertical feet skied. Starting at 8:30 A.M., they rode the tram twenty-five times before 4 P.M., skiing a total of 103,475 vertical feet.

Recalls Bruce Morley, "Pepi was going to join us that day, but his Porsche wouldn't start, so he missed the first tram."

Stiegler, however, got all the snow he could handle in the early years. "We had the best powder skiing of all times," he says, with palpable nostalgia in his voice. "You have no idea. All the employees knew where the best powder was. Nobody else knew where to go. Maybe some locals. We employees had a feast, a powder feast. We actually considered it our personal mountain."

In some ways, Jackson Hole was a fiefdom, where the feudal lord huddled in his office, poring over account books, while the serfs had the run of the countryside. By day, there was

Left: Pepi Stiegler, who personally removed the trees from Pepi's Run on Sublette Ridge. Above: Jorge Colón, who has many first descents in the Tetons to his name. Above right: Pioneering monoskier Mike Doyle. Right: Après Ski, 70s style.

endless powder, still fresh two or three days after a storm, and by night, endless parties. Gene Downer, founder of the Figure Eight competition, remembers a skinny-dipping party in the pool of the Sojourner Inn that raged all night. Finally a guest threw open his window and shouted down to the darkened pool, "If you don't shut up, I'm going to call the manager!"

At that moment, Sojourner employee Ertz Gross, naked, was on the diving board. "I am the manager!" he shouted back, then dove in.

The customers fared little better on the mountain. As Stiegler says, "The ski bums ruled the tram." McCollister, ever mindful of the difference between genuine guests and local ski bums, had instituted a system of A passes and B passes. The B pass was several hundred dollars cheaper but required holders to stand in a separate line, underneath the tram dock, and provided only standby tram privileges. This, however, hardly mattered, since the B pass holders were usually the ones riding the tram.

"Tourists getting on the tram would ask, 'Is it okay to step in here?'" says Stiegler. "There were some complaints. Paul got pretty upset about that."

When Paul McCollister and Alex Morley planned Teton Village, they envisioned a European-style ski hamlet, where residents lived over their shops and lodges housed both guests and employees. When the ski resort opened for the 1965-66 season, their vision had been realized, albeit on a small scale. Besides the clock tower and tram building, the Seven Levels Inn, the Alpenhof, and the Sojourner Inn were all that existed, each fitting the village's quaint, continental paradigm.

But the European Alps are scattered with more than just pricey chalets and inns; there are also large mountain huts (or refuges), where hikers, climbers, and skiers can find cheap beds and good fellowship. Colby Wilson envisioned just such a place when he came with his family to Jackson Hole in the summer of 1966. After riding the tram up and down Rendezvous Mountain, the family was lunching in the cafeteria when Wilson suddenly got up and disappeared. He came back in an hour, announcing he'd taken an option on a nearby building site for a hotel.

As his son Benny Wilson explains, "My dad was sick of going to different ski areas with five kids and having to pay a lot of money at hotels. So he said, 'I'm going to build my own hotel, and we'll never have to travel to another ski area again.' "

The Hostel X
JACKSON HOLE'S INSTITUTION

Robert Trent Smith redesigned the course this spring, adding a gaping sand trap on the first and fifth holes . . . Wilson points out that the nine-hole layout is designed for the five, six and seven iron. In fact, players are required to putt with a seven iron . . . Although Wilson refused comment, rumor has it that the country club will apply for a limited retail liquor license as soon as the course has been recognized by the United States Golf Association." Wilson's eldest son, Mike, who runs the hostel today, remembers, "People started stopping by with their golf clubs, asking where the course was."

Paul McCollister, according to Benny and Mike Wilson, didn't always appreciate the hostel's less-than-luxurious image, and Wilson didn't always appreciate McCollister's controlling nature or frugality. A few times their differences came to a head, as when Wilson demolished McCollister's dog pound or engaged in some illicit landscaping.

As Mike Wilson remembers, "Paul McCollister refused to pave the

Teton Village's most affordable accomodations.

That fall Wilson built the Hostel X, so named because each room originally cost ten dollars. It added sixty-five rooms to Teton Village, which had had a total of only eighty-two before then. (Also constructed in time for the 1966-67 season were the Mangy Moose Saloon and the Holten Inn, now the Inn of Jackson Hole.) With its large, open spaces and instant appeal to ski bums, the hostel won rave reviews. In 1971, SKI Magazine called it "Jackson's greatest institution."

Colby Wilson was a habitual prankster. Behind the hostel's front desk are two embroidered signs, made by a guest, that permanently give "Colby's forecast." One says, "Snow tonight." The other, "Sun tomorrow." Wilson used to have a dish of candy on the desk with a sign that read, "One for ten cents, two for a quarter."

In the autumn of 1975, Wilson laid out a Lilliputian golf course behind the hostel and persuaded the Jackson Hole News to write it up as if it were the real thing. As the paper reported, "Club professional Colby Wilson explained that nationally known course architect

roads or the parking lot. There was a hole in the main road, probably two or three feet deep. So my dad decided to do something about it. One morning, Paul came driving down the road, headed for his office, and there was a tree planted in the hole. It was a good-sized tree, too, five or six feet tall."

Though Colby Wilson died in 1998, at the age of seventy-six, and Mike, fifty-five, now charges a bit more per room than his father used to (forty-eight dollars for two), the Hostel X continues to be an institution. Ski racing teams still fill its rooms during the Wild West Classic, just as they did in the late 1960s, and Mike still occasionally projects Ski the Outer Limits and Rhythms, some of the classic sixteen-millimeter films in the hostel's collection. Watching the movies in the hostel's basement, the walls plastered with ski posters, one senses that the hostel is both museum and lodge, upholding Jackson Hole's proud ski-bum heritage and still proving that skiing need not be a rich man's game.

Left: Skiing the Inn roof, a Jackson Hole tradition.
Below: Ski School in the late 1960s, when low-cut ski boots met high fashion, particularly on the smallest skiers

"The B pass line was definitely a sub-culture unto its own," says Benny Wilson. Now a ski instructor, Wilson grew up in Teton Village. His father, Colby Wilson, started the Hostel X, so named because every room, whether inhabited by one person or four, cost ten dollars per night. At the opposite end of the spectrum from Dick and Anneliese Oberreit's sophisticated, European-flavored Alpenhof, the Hostel X was—and still is—the nucleus of Jackson Hole's ski bum scene. When ski films came to Jackson Hole, they usually premiered in the Hostel basement, which was also famous for Tuesday night fondue parties.

Colby Wilson was also famed for his clashes with McCollister. After an incident in which two roving Saint Bernards devoured a wealthy guest's miniature poodle, McCollister had banned all dogs from Teton Village. He'd even built his own "pound," a large steel cage that he kept behind the maintenance shop. When Benny Wilson's dog Elvis disappeared, the elder Wilson found him in McCollister's cage. With an eight-pound sledgeham-mer, Wilson demolished the cage, then dragged the remnants in front of the ski resort's administrative offices and left them there.

Above: Paul Huser leaves a contrail. Right: If you are nonchalantly handed such a patch, you are officially a member of the Jackson Hole Air Force.

Benny Wilson shares his father's iconoclastic character. Returning from a stint in the Marines, he decided that if Jackson Hole's slopes were skied out, he'd ski roofs instead. "One night at Mangy Moose, George Hufsmith and I were contemplating how bumps were prevalent everywhere on the mountain," Wilson recalls. "As we were looking out the windows, we noticed that the roof of the Inn of Jackson Hole had perfectly smooth snow, and the angle was just like the mountain itself. We still had all our ski gear on, so we finished our drinks, got a ladder from the hostel, climbed up the roof's chimney line so we wouldn't ruin where we were going to ski, then skied down, went back in the Moose, and had more drinks."

Since then, skiing the Inn roof has become a tradition, upheld yearly by a few skiers willing to brave the end-of-the-run jump to the ground. It's not the only tradition inspired by alcohol. Sharing a similarly well-lubricated origin is the Jackson Hole Air Force, a loose-knit society of hardcore locals that Wilson founded and named during a lengthy blizzard in 1984.

"The tram had been closed for a bunch of days and we were getting really bored," he explains. "We were sitting in the Bear Claw Café

[now the Village Café] gelande quaffing—somebody would slide a full beer off the end of the bar and you'd have to catch it in midair and drink it. We started thinking about parties we could have when the tram opened up again, and that's when we came up with the Jackson Hole Air Force."

Today the Air Force is about a hundred members strong. But in the beginning, it was just a small group of locals bound by their love of aggressive, exploratory skiing. Says Wilson:

"It was basically just about skiing deep powder with your friends, taking big air, and skiing in places nobody else would want to. Going OB was no big deal—we'd even send back reports to the patrol about avalanche conditions."

In the ensuing years, however, the ski patrol, under the longtime directorship of Dean Moore, began to clamp down on Air Force members and other locals who snuck under boundary ropes to "poach" the backcountry. The worry was that tourists would heedlessly follow their tracks into avalanche terrain. Adopting the motto, "swift, silent, deep" (a play on the "swift, silent, deadly" motto of the U.S. Marines' First Battalion), the Air Force took on more clandes-

In the late-1960s, ski photographers could shoot inbounds and still find nearly untracked powder all day.

tine connotations. Ironically, it also gained a measure of fame. Ski magazines lionized the Air Force, making much of its members' secrecy and the military-style patches they wore on their parkas.

The growing fascination with Jackson Hole's rebellious spirit was a reflection of the resort's increasing success. Harry Baxter's relentless promotions and sales calls on tour operators and travel agents were paying off. In 1985, Paul McCollister inked a deal with American Airlines to provide charter flights to Jackson Hole from Chicago and Dallas. In 1988, the *Jackson Hole News* ran an article, "Winter Economy Surges to Record," which reported that the ski area would log 230,000 skier days that season, 17.2 percent more than the previous year. A chamber of commerce executive gushed: "The word is out that Jackson Hole is the hot spot."

McCollister had succeeded where many thought he would fail, as Alex Morley was willing to concede. "I came back to Jackson and went skiing with Paul," says Morley. "We were riding the lift and I said, 'Paul, I've got to compliment you. I never imagined you would be able to hang on this long.' He said, 'You know, I'm just like a bulldog. I've got ahold of this thing,

Austrian Franz Klammer in the 1975 World Series Downhill, skiing in the downhill (left) and dual slalom (below). Klammer broke the downhill course record on his final run with a time of 1:55.64, a record that still stands as the course has not been used since.

and I'm going to hang on to it.'"

But McCollister needed more than mere mettle to ensure further success. Improvements to the ski area had been few and infrequent. In 1970 the Thunder Lift was added, so guests would not have to ski Rendezvous Mountain top to bottom each time they went to the summit, and in 1974 the Casper Lift gave beginners and intermediates an alternative to Après Vous. But the resort repeatedly drew low ratings from ski magazines for its antiquated lifts, grooming, and snowmaking.

Even racing, so close to McCollister's heart, had fallen by the wayside. The last major race, the 1975 World Series Downhill, was plagued by problems: A storm dumped several feet of snow, and the resort's rudimentary snowcats couldn't efficiently clear the course. This was, Pepi Stiegler suspects, one reason the Russian delegates cast the deciding vote against Jackson Hole during its bid for the 1978 World Championships, handing the event instead to Garmisch. After that defeat, McCollister gave up his ambition to host international races.

It was, in some ways, unfortunate. Jackson Hole's downhill course was extraordinary. Starting on the East Ridge just below the summit of Rendezvous, the route crossed Tensleep Bowl, plunged

down the steep, narrow Downhill Chute, then streaked down Amphitheater and Gros Ventre to the valley floor. In the 1975 race, Franz Klammer delighted spectators by breaking the course record, finishing in one minute, 55.64 seconds. But the races drained resources, and the course split the mountain in two, seriously disrupting resort operations. As McCollister admitted, "Ski racing was a lot of fun, but it was very expensive and unpopular with destination skiers."

Far more popular, McCollister knew, were high-speed quads and flawlessly groomed runs. In the late 1980s, he began casting about for ways to raise four million dollars for such improvements. Two Austrian families, the Von Finks and Von Eikels, whose

fortunes came from banking and brewing, were eager to invest, but McCollister turned them down, worried they'd try to incorporate Jackson Hole Ski Corporation into their empire. Instead, he turned to Dutch oil baron John Deuss, who vacationed frequently at Teton Village. In the spring of 1987, McCollister flew to New York to broker a deal with Deuss, but, as usual, ignored advice to proceed cautiously.

According to Steve Duerr, McCollister's in-house lawyer from 1986 to 1992, "I lined up

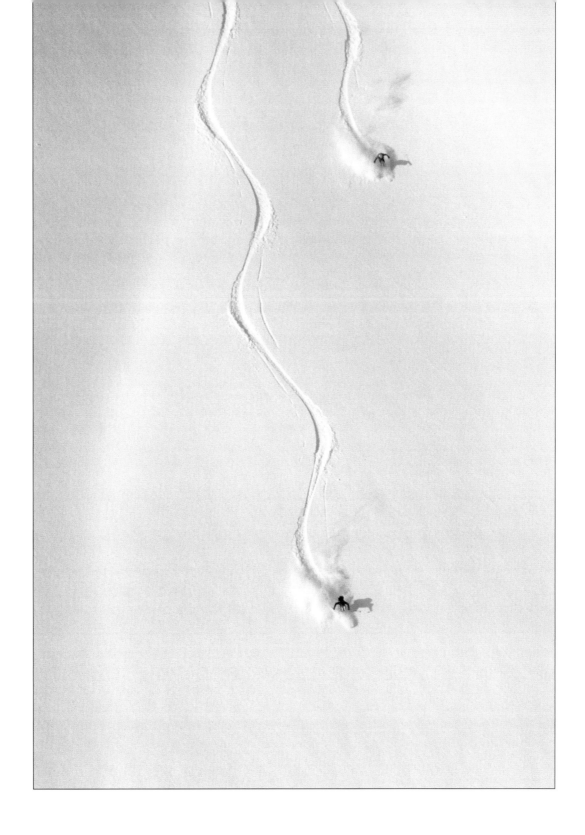

New York counsel to go with Paul. Instead, he flew from New York in a helicopter to Philadelphia [where Deuss had another office]. Basically, Paul cut a deal with John Deuss to get 3.6 million bucks, just the two of them, agreeing on a handshake. Deuss then confirmed it with a six-page letter explaining their agreement."

The letter would become the object of five years of contention, frustration, and legal jousting. As soon as he had Deuss's agreement, McCollister installed the Sublette quad and a snowmaking system. He also bought heavy machinery with which to smooth out rocky slopes and reduce breakovers—"summer grooming," as it's called. The money was gone by the fall of 1987, when McCollister and Deuss began to argue over the letter's meaning. In short, Deuss had given McCollister the $3.6 million in exchange for equity. In turn, McCollister had agreed to part with 24 percent of the company's stock, with provisions for Deuss's equity to increase if the company did not perform well. To insure he stayed in control, McCollister insisted on a guarantee that Deuss could gain no more than 49 percent of the corporation. But he miscalculated. His own stock holding totalled only 63 percent. If Deuss gained 49 percent of

the company's stock, which was likely, McCollister's shares would drop to 32 percent, making Deuss majority owner. This was anathema to McCollister, according to his son Mike.

"Dad couldn't give up control," says the younger McCollister, who worked with his father for fourteen years as mountain manager. "He was a very controlling guy."

Moreover, the agreement stipulated that the corporation's real estate assets be transferred to another corporation, which would have resulted in $7.2 million in taxes. McCollister himself would have owed $2 million. Not only would he lose control of the company he'd struggled to keep afloat for two

decades, he'd also be plunged into debt. Naturally he balked.

And Deuss sued. Not that he needed the money. John Deuss was a self-made billionaire who'd made his fortune wheeling and dealing on the international crude oil market. According to the *Jackson Hole News*, not long before he sued the Jackson Hole Ski Corporation, Deuss nearly cornered the market for North Sea crude oil. Earlier, in the late '70s and early '80s, he'd been one of the principal oil

suppliers to South Africa, earning an estimated $300–$500 million on commissions, despite a United Nations embargo. The Ski Corp stock he'd sued for amounted to little more than Wyoming chicken feed to Deuss, but the matter, it can be assumed, had become personal. On January 1, 1988, while on a Jackson Hole ski vacation, Deuss met McCollister in his office to sort out the situation. It didn't go well. At the climax of the meeting, it was reported, Deuss spat at McCollister, "You're on a different planet."

For four years, the battle raged, in the courtrooms and in the pages of Jackson Hole's newspapers. First Deuss won an injunction that froze the resort's assets and prohibited it from incurring any more debt. This quashed any plans for further improvements and made daily operation difficult. Then Deuss won a summary judgment, forcing McCollister to hand over the stock in question. McCollister gained a little time when the Federal Circuit Court of Appeals in Denver overturned the judgment, but by then he was heavily in debt, due to legal fees.

Hoping to regain his financial footing, McCollister took a major gamble. On a Teton Village lot at the base of the tram's Tower

One, he planned a townhouse development that would earn enough to pay off Deuss.

Says Steve Duerr, "Typical of his nature, he moved quickly on some sketchy architectural plans and got people building. He ended getting about a million dollars in debt. And who does he go to when he needs more money? August Von Fink."

Von Fink was the Austrian billionaire who'd wanted to invest in the Ski Corp in the mid-1980s, only to be turned down by McCollister. According to the *News*, construction loans that McCollister was able to obtain from the German banking house of Merck, Fink eventually topped out at ten million dollars, but only seven

of the twelve units in phase one of the Tramtower Townhouses were sold. On his last roll of the dice, McCollister had lost. "The loan on Tramtower was devastating," McCollister told the *News*. "That was the problem, not the litigation."

"We tried to find a white knight to wade in here and solve this," says Duerr, "and we finally did—John Resor."

One of the Resor clan that owns Snake River Ranch, adjacent to Teton Village, John Resor was a canny, Yale-educated businessman

Facing page: Dirk Collins
in the Crags. This page:
Teton Village, the name
local skiers often give for
the ski resort as well.

who'd been interested for several years in buying McCollister's stake in the Jackson Hole Ski Corporation. All attempts to make a deal with McCollister had fallen through. Alternatively, he turned to John Deuss, but efforts to orchestrate a deal with the Dutch oilman also failed. As another McCollister-Deuss trial date neared, Resor thought he'd lost his opportunity. Then a friend, Jerry Rankin, introduced Resor to John "Jay" Kemmerer III, member of a famous Wyoming coal-mining family.

In 1897, Mahlon Kemmerer founded the western Wyoming town that bears his name, having established a coal mining operation nearby. In 1981, his descendants sold the mine to a subsidiary of Gulf Oil for $325 million. A decade later, Jay Kemmerer, chair of the Kemmerer Family Trust, was anxious to reinvest in the state so closely tied to his family's history. The McCollister-Deuss entanglement intrigued him; the property in question was just the sort of Wyoming investment the Kemmerers wanted. When Resor met with Deuss in a New York hotel room on June 30, 1992, Jay Kemmerer was with him.

Doggedly pursuing a deal, Resor negotiated far into the night with Kemmerer's and Deuss's representatives. Finally, at 2:30 A.M., the

Below: Paul McCollister, photographed in 1991, the year before he sold the ski resort. Right: Bald eagle and alpenglow.

two sides reached an agreement, the final step in a complex transaction that had Kemmerer buying out both Deuss and McCollister while also paying off McCollister's personal debt to Merck, Fink. As for Resor, he would become the resort's new CEO.

It was the beginning of the Kemmerer era at Jackson Hole, and the end of a long, rough road for McCollister, who was seventy-seven at the time. True to character, he shrugged off the loss. In a press conference he said, "I am glad to get rid of the litigation and the other albatross [the Tramtower debt]. It's kind of like getting rid of your kid. It's a part of you, but I will get over it." According to his friends and family, he never did.

"It was a major blow," says Mike McCollister. "The ski resort was so important to him. It was his creation, his child, his baby."

When McCollister died in 1999 at the age of eighty-three, an extravagant vision for Jackson Hole ski resort died with him. As long as he owned the resort, he had also hoped to build another small, high-altitude village in Rock Springs Canyon, south of the ski area. In the manner of "ski stations" in the French and Swiss Alps, it would be connected to Teton Village by cog railway.

"That was one of the dreams that was so important to him," says Mike McCollister. "I thought it was ridiculous from an environmental standpoint. And it would be right at the bottom of a humungous slide path. But he always wanted to do it. Once Dad got an idea in his head, he didn't let go."

That may be the salient characteristic of all of the figures who've made their mark on the Tetons. For McCollister, the most vital goal was that Jackson Hole ski resort would succeed. In the wake of his tribulations, it has, under Jay Kemmerer. But McCollister's own success cannot be demeaned.

Though he considers his tenure with McCollister the hardest five years of his life, Steve Duerr remembers McCollister fondly. "There's a book about the pioneers, *Men to Match My Mountains*," says Duerr. "McCollister was that person. He was up to the challenge of getting a million-dollar loan to put a tram from a hayfield to the top of a mountain five hundred miles from any population base, with no transportation to speak of. And he succeeded. That's pretty gutsy, pretty tenacious. I'd say he matched the mountain."

chapter 5

PATROLLING THE HOLE

Greg Miles dug into his backpack and from it extracted a bright orange, two-pound explosive charge shaped like a soda can. With black electrical tape he lashed the charge, which is meant to release potential avalanches and settle the new snow, to a six-foot piece of bamboo.

"You hang here," he said. "Keep an eye on me. When this touches off, grab that second piece of 'boo and 'Z' down this slope to me." With his "stick bomb" under his arm, he turned and traversed the slope below.

We were at the top of Casper Bowl, a steep basin of crags and chutes far above any lifts. We'd hiked there before dawn from the upper terminal of the Bridger Gondola. As the sun rose, the previous night's storm clouds began to burn off. Newly crowned by eight inches of snow, Rendezvous Mountain's ridges, trees, and cliffs gradually emerged from the murk. Everything was stenciled in pale sunshine. But if any of the dozen patrollers who were fanned out across Casper Bowl noticed the fine morning light, they didn't say so. Instead, their radios crackled with the clipped dialogue of men and women engrossed by physical, technical, and possibly deadly work.

"Mountain station, route 7-A is clear of the road cut."

"Air blast, shot 14, Casper, one hundred seconds."

Wham. A bag of explosive charges that had been trollied along a line strung between Casper Bowl's cliffs detonated, the echo rolling down the mountain. A cloud of powder billowed into the air, and a tongue of crumbled snow slid out from between two crags.

"Expert chutes, bomb trolley, sixty seconds."

Elsewhere on the mountain, explosives thumped and boomed. Many of the detonations were invisible from my vantage point. But I could see several patrollers working their way down Casper Bowl, throwing explosives and watching each other closely, like a platoon of infantrymen moving cautiously across a steep, white, no man's land.

My own duty was to keep a close eye on Greg Miles, a 13-year patroller who came to Jackson for one winter twenty years ago and stayed. Planting the stick bomb in a gully thirty yards below, Greg yelled up at me: "Once I pull this igniter, it'll be sixty seconds before it goes off. You'll want to cover your ears."

Fitting an igniter to the fuse, he shouted across the bowl, "Air blast, sixty

Mark Newcomb winds up before throwing a one-pound hand charge into
Rendezvous Bowl. Tucked into his sunglass strap is a wind-proof igniter.

Right: Greg Miles climbs the Headwall before sunrise.

seconds!" Then he bellowed, "Fire in the hole!" yanked the igniter, and scooted across the gully to the safety of a clump of trees.

I clamped my hands over my ears. Just before the charge detonated, it occurred to me that this was, indeed, probably the closest I would ever come to war. But to Greg and his fellow patrollers, it was just another day at the office.

Everything that makes Jackson Hole Mountain Resort a great ski area—the huge bowls, steep ridges, and narrow slots—also makes it an exceptionally difficult place to keep safe. Just as in a military campaign, patrolling entails constant surveillance, precise tactics, even heavy artillery. It is, without question, the most exciting

Left and above: Detonated by the ski patrol in January, 1996,
this avalanche was featured in the opening few moments of both Teton Gravity Research's *The Continuum*.

and prestigious job a patroller can have in this country. And the fifty-six men and women of the Jackson Hole Ski Patrol know it—they're a cocky, close-knit bunch who revel in their history. Most have been on the patrol for more than a decade; some for more than three decades. In a job that constantly pits its practitioners against biting temperatures and hazardous conditions, that's an uncommon commitment. But theirs is an uncommon workplace.

"It's the mountain that keeps us here," says patrol director Corky Ward, who's been on the job since 1974. "It challenges us on a daily basis and keeps us well in tune. Even if it hasn't snowed in three weeks, you can't let your guard down. On many ski mountains, if you don't have snow, you have bored patrolmen, and if you have bored patrolmen you have bickering, infighting, so forth and so on. This mountain just doesn't allow that."

A lack of snow, however, is not something that Jackson patrollers often deal with. The three–to five hundred inches of light, dry, unstable snow that fall annually on Rendezvous Mountain, coupled with nearly two hundred avalanche paths, have made the Jackson Hole Ski Patrol what it is today.

Right: Patrollers make
their morning commute
to Mountain Station, their
office in Corbet's Cabin.
Below: Patrol Director
Corky Ward.

When the resort began operation in 1965, ski-
area avalanche control was still a young science. Most
modern techniques were developed after World War II
at steep, snowy Alta ski resort in Utah. Because the
National Guard armory in Salt Lake City was nearby,
snow-science pioneers Ed LaChapelle and Monty
Atwater were able to experiment with howitzers and
hand charges to settle Alta's slopes.

When the Forest Service granted the permit
to the fledgling Jackson Hole ski resort, it sent LaChapelle
to Wyoming to lay out Rendezvous Mountain's snow-control

Above: Patrollers "wrap" charges, inserting fuses into the explosive material then securing them with black electrical tape. Above right: Kirby Williams. Right: On stormy mornings, patrollers indulge their dark sense of humor by uncovering select words on the sign at the top of the aerial tram.

SAFETY MESSAGE

routes and artillery placements. His innovations would be tested on an unprecedented scale, though not immediately. With the tram still under construction during the 1965-66 season, the fifteen patrollers under then-Patrol Director Frank Ewing's leadership had little to do.

"We had three to four times as many patrollers as we needed, with only Après Vous open," recalls Rod Newcomb, who had been hired as one of Jackson Hole's first patrollers after cutting the trees for the Teewinot lift line.

Everything changed the next year. With the tram open, the skiable terrain tripled in size. Having done similar work at Squaw Valley, Latvian-born Juris Krisjansons became the local Forest Service snow ranger, responsible for avalanche forecasting and directing snow control. Newcomb, who'd patrolled previously at Alta, became his assistant. A dozen more patrollers were hired, though many hardly knew what they were up against.

"The first year the tram was open was a real learning experience," says Newcomb, who founded the American Avalanche Institute after his five-year tenure as assistant snow ranger. "I don't think all the patrollers agreed with our policy of saturation bombing. They thought a lot of stuff

Left: Assistant Snow Ranger Rod Newcomb in the resort's early years, with one of the ski area's three army surplus radios in his pack. Right: First Patrol Director Frank Ewing and Snow Ranger Juris Krisjansons with a 75 millimeter recoilless rifle, which used World War II-era ordnance.

could be skied, but these people hadn't come from a class-A avalanche ski area. A nucleus of patrollers who came from Alta—Kent Hoopingarner, Lonnie Ball, Gary Poulson—they understood."

Everybody else soon learned what was at stake. Early that winter, in December 1966, patroller Dick Porter traversed into a gully (now known as Dick's Ditch) that avalanched on top of him. His coworkers probed for an hour before Pete Lev's pole hit Porter's ski. Miraculously, he was still alive, though literally blue when he was dug out. Porter was rushed to the bottom, where local physician "Doc" Walker thawed him with successively warmer baths in the Seven Levels Inn.

As the patrol gained experience, they honed their tools and invented new ones. Krisjansons developed the first on-mountain weather instrumentation of its kind in the Rockies. His successor, Gary Poulson, invented a closed-circuit TV system to gauge the previous night's snowfall. With great success, the patrollers tested stick bombs and bomb trolleys, which allow charges to detonate in midair, spreading the impact.

One important innovation came out

of the ski patrol's most tragic season. On December 3, 1985, before the resort had opened for the season, six patrollers were skiing down the east side of Rendezvous Bowl when the slope fractured. Grabbing hold of trees or swimming atop the rumbling, tumbling slabs of snow, five of the patrollers escaped. Paul Driscoll, buried under five feet of snow at the bottom of the slide path, didn't.

In the wake of this fatality—the ski patrol's first—Jim Kanzler devised the "big

bomb," an idea since borrowed by many other ski areas. Patrollers piled fifty pounds of explosives into a plastic kiddie sled, lowered it into Rendezvous Bowl, and then detonated it from afar. The blast started an avalanche that scoured the bowl bare and slid 1,300 feet into Cheyenne Gully.

But the patrollers' revenge on the snowpack was short-lived. In February, a massive storm dumped nearly six feet of snow on the mountain in six days.

"We'd never been in that scenario before," recalls Kirby Williams, who's been patrolling since the tram opened. "We didn't know how to deal with it."

On February 17, 1986, patrollers bombarded Moran Face with

hand charges and artillery shells. Still worried about the slope's safety, Paul Rice, John Bernadyn, and Tom Raymer went back to do their control route again. After throwing several more explosives, Raymer traversed under the face. Only then did the slope fracture, fatally burying him under twelve feet of snow. His fellow patrollers were devastated.

"We shouldn't have been out there at all," says Williams, who took the two deaths particularly hard and sat out the next season. "After such a storm, you wait. We learned a hard lesson."

Today, Tom Raymer's name lives on in the Raymer snow-study plot on the Headwall, where avalanche forecasters gather much of their data, and in his cabin on the Village Road. Donated by his family after

his death, the cabin serves as accommodations for visiting ski patrollers on exchange. Raymer and Driscoll are also memorialized each February with an après-ski remembrance—some might call it a drunken bash—in the patrol locker room.

The fateful 1985-86 season was particularly dramatic. Only a few days after Raymer's death, Kirby Williams fired a shell from the patrollers' 105-millimeter recoilless rifle that set off an avalanche on the Headwall.

Facing page and left: Rod Newcomb and Frank Ewing load and fire a World War I era "pack" howitzer (so-called because it could be disassembled and packed on horses) at the ski area's lower faces. Above: Shells for the 75-millimeter recoilless rifle were kept in a bunker under the gun placement.

Fracturing six feet deep, the slide ran all the way down Amphitheater, ripping out two new restrooms and a warming hut, blasting through lower Tramline, and depositing the wreckage only a few hundred feet from homes at the base of the mountain. The slide was so monstrous that patroller Renny Jackson, pulling into the Teton Village parking lot on his way to work, got out of his car and began backing away when he saw it coming.

Apart from that climactic season, Jackson Hole's patrollers were unaccustomed to death and destruction. Williams, for one, recalls the early years nostalgically. "It could be my imagination," he says, "but it seems like it just snowed and snowed and snowed back in those days. And there was nobody here. We were basically in a pioneer situation, with a new mountain that was so cool, so big, with all that snow, and we didn't have to share it with very many people. It was a ski bum's dream. Back in the old days, we'd straighten a few barricades, throw a few bombs, and ski the shit out of it."

The patrollers skied in rat packs of seven or eight, finding fresh snow in the Alta Chutes, Tower Three Chutes, and Hobacks as much as three days after a storm. Few skiers on the hill meant there were few

Rod Newcomb aims the 75 millimeter recoilless rifle, which stood near the aerial tram's Tower Three. On the laminated sheet under the rifle is a chart of targeting coordinates.

accidents to respond to, and training was limited to one session in the fall and one or two lift-evacuation drills during the winter.

"On a wing and a prayer was the attitude," says Williams. "We made it work because we had a lot of young, talented guys. We just flat skied a lot. And we drank a lot, too."

The patrollers' favorite place to imbibe was their own locker room, known as Bernie's Boom Boom Room, after John "Bernie" Bernadyn. An electrical engineer who came to Jackson Hole to design the aerial tram's control system, Bernadyn stayed on and joined the patrol. A lifelong bachelor, Bernie held court during drinking sessions in the Boom Boom Room until his retirement, in 1996, at the age of seventy.

"We used to have a keg down there, on tap all the time," says Robert Nelson, 62, who has been patrolling as long as Williams. "You could get a 'season pass' for 125 bucks and drink all the beer you wanted during the season. That hurt a lot of people."

Today, the keg is gone but the camaraderie lives on. You can see it in the patrollers' idiosyncratic lingo—responding to an accident is "running a wreck"; a patroller stationed atop Rendezvous is a "big hill worker"; a dusting of

Jackson's Four-Legged Patrollers

mental in saving an avalanche victim. In just a few minutes, Coup had justified twelve years of hard work and training.

In 1980, few ski areas in the West had instituted avalanche dog programs, relying only on probe lines—a row of rescuers standing shoulder to shoulder, probing into the snow with long poles—to find avalanche victims. Patroller Peter MacKay knew dogs could do a better job. That year he established the resort's avy dog program, with a female black lab named Seal. Such dogs are still used today—females don't fight and don't mark their territories, and labs and other sporting breeds work fast and can take orders from different people (as opposed to German Shepherds, say, who work methodically and follow only one master). Labs and retrievers are also relatively light, the better to be carried on a patroller's shoulders or towed in a toboggan.

"One trained dog is worth, basically, 200 to 300 probers," MacKay told *Jackson Hole* Magazine in 1996. "There's no ifs, ands, or buts about it."

Today there are six dogs on patrol—Moon Pie, Kedar, Peppercorn, Bailey, Deuce, and Mojo (who work with patrollers Balint, Mr. Nelson, Jake Elkins, Glen Jaques, Carrie Cook, and Dick Frost, respectively). They can mostly be found in their crates in the Boom Boom Room, or in Corbet's Cabin, lounging on the couch in Mountain Station, the patrollers' office.

"If need be, we'll run 'em," says Balint, "But we usually don't. We want them to be fresh when we get to the scene."

Canine Corps

On April 3, 1992, a new hero was made at Jackson Hole. That morning, Robert "Drew" Dunlap and some friends went to ski corn in the backcountry south of Jackson Hole Mountain Resort. The snow, however, hadn't frozen hard the night before, and even though Dunlap's party was at the top of their last run by 10 a.m., avalanche conditions were already ripe. When Dunlap dropped off the top of a ridge into Green River Canyon, a huge avalanche broke loose, carrying him for nine hundred feet, then burying him under four feet of heavy, wet snow.

An hour and a half later, patrollers Jerry Balint and Jake Elkins and avalanche dogs Coup and Barley Corn were at the scene, brought in by helicopter. Minutes later, both dogs had smelled something under the snow, and a muffled yell was heard. All the rescuers were pulled off, and Coup was sent in alone. Digging frantically, the female black lab uncovered Dunlap's cold but relieved face.

This was the first time in North America a dog had been instru-

It is, by all appearances, a life of leisure. But these dogs are pros. Anytime an avalanche occurs in the region—in Grand Teton National Park, at Yellowstone, on Teton Pass—one or two Jackson Hole dogs are soon on the way in by helicopter. And their skills have taken some of them even farther.

"I've hauled Moon Pie five times to the World Extreme Skiing Championships in Valdez, Alaska," says Balint.

When called on for a search, however, the dogs don't usually have a chance to be heroes. It's extremely rare for a victim to survive under the snow for ninety-two minutes, as Dunlap did. Avalanches often mangle their victims, killing them immediately, or they occur too far out in the backcountry for help to arrive quickly enough. Jackson Hole's dogs have sped up several body recoveries, but not since Coup's famous find has an avy dog saved a life.

Then again, this is Jackson Hole, where skiers are constantly testing the snowpack's limits, and where it may not be long before another buried skier is greeted by the joyful sight of a wet, black nose.

Left: Mark Wolling tosses a two-pound charge into the upper slopes of Tensleep Bowl. Above: Glen Jacques looks on as his dog makes a find.

powder on a freshly groomed run is "cowboy pow"—and in the nicknames they've bestowed on each other. Sparky, Skin, Hubba Bubba, Ali Bob, Bevis, Doodle, Two Dogs, Goober, Cookie, Chuckie, The Fat, The Oralator, Smiley, Olive Oil, Droodle, Gunner Girl, Goldie, Frosty, Romeo, The Cow, Gros Ventre, and Big Wally are some of the more polite examples.

Most of the nicknames are riffs on names, appearances, or personalities. Jim Springer is Spring Loose; Glen Jacques, known for wearing sunglasses inside, is Blind Glen. And veteran Gerry Amadon, "who likes to tell ya how to do it," is Coach.

Some patrollers bear two nicknames. Born in southern

Wyoming, Robert Nelson was long ago nicknamed Herder for that region's history of sheepherding. But most current ski resort employees know him only as Mr. Nelson. Today this name is a gesture of respect, but it didn't quite start out that way.

Recalls Nelson, "Years ago, Holly McCollister [Paul's daughter, in charge of human resources] wrote a memo that said that whenever you answered the phone, you were supposed to call yourself Mr., then say your

Tom Russo reaches back to hurl a charge into Corbet's Couloir. Russo and his fellow patrollers on snow control route 4 rappel or jump into Corbet's nearly every day in the season. Left: Robert Nelson.

department. So I started answering the phone like the memo said—'This is Mr. Nelson from ski patrol.' The workers got a kick out of that, and the name stuck. Anyway, there are too many Bobs on patrol."

The patrol's camaraderie is also reflected in its "literary heritage." A few years ago, just before evening sweep, Mr. Nelson recited a poem into his radio. The practice caught on, and now it's an implied duty for the Après Vous and gondola patrollers to broadcast a new poem each afternoon. Every ski-resort employee with a walkie-talkie tunes in at 4:20 P.M. to hear the verses, which usually reflect the day's events—the

Above: Juris Krisjansons watches the blast from a hand charge. Below: Mark Wolling. Facing page: A natural slide on No Name Peak in 1999 resulted in a "crown," or upper fracture line, twelve feet deep.

wrecks run, the snow conditions, or whatever else might stir a patroller's poetic muse.

"The panty tree is a sight to see," began a recent offering by the Après Vous crew about the famous underwear-bedecked aspen under the high-speed quad. "The garments are growing geometrically."

The jokes, however, stop short when storms roll in across the Tetons, digging their gray fingers into every canyon and cirque. When the snow falls heavy and wet, and western winds dangerously load Rendezvous's east-facing slopes, the situation must be handled with a combination of careful thought, military precision, and brute force.

Early in the season or on days of extreme avalanche danger, the battle begins at 5 A.M. With a 105 millimeter howitzer located near the mountain's base, gunner Todd Harley lobs explosive shells at Sheridan Bowl, the Crags, and Moran Faces. Soon after, a handful of patrollers is scattered across the mountain, manning "avalaunchers" (compressed-nitrogen-powered rifles) and firing explosives at the Expert Chutes, Pepi's Bench, and the Headwall.

In midwinter, the rest of the patrollers,

as well as two or three avalanche dogs (see page 101), arrive at the top of the tram just as dawn breaks. It can be a near-apocalyptic scene, with winds caterwauling through the tram dock's steel latticework and patrollers plodding through the driven snow to Mountain Station, their mountaintop office in Corbet's Cabin.

Once inside, they move fast, shoving hand charges affixed with long, white fuses into their packs; checking the signals from each other's avalanche transceivers; and receiving last-minute instructions from avalanche-reduction leader Greg Martell, who decides the scope and emphasis of the morning's control work. Then they're out the door, in groups of three or four, to cover

Above: Corky Ward fires the 105 millimeter recoilless rifle in the predawn darkness. Left: Jerry Balint and Peter Barker load the 75 millimeter recoilless rifle.

eight control routes, intricately orchestrated so that the patrollers can constantly check on each other and ferret out as many potential slides as possible.

Contrary to what jealous skiers in the tram line at the bottom of the mountain may think, there's little powder skiing on a snow control route—it's mainly traverse, wait, listen, signal to other patrollers, traverse again. There is, however, plenty of firepower. On a high-danger day, gunners may fire twenty-five shells and other patrollers may deploy up to two hundred hand charges, all before the resort opens at 9 A.M.

Says Corky Ward with certain pride, "Even on a high-hazard

day we can cover 95 percent of all the avalanche paths on the mountain in an hour and a half."

Although preventing avalanches and erecting barricades have long been the patrol's bread-and-butter, the situation is gradually evolving. Unlike other resorts in the Rockies, Jackson Hole's slopes are generally uncrowded and most of its skiers are proficient, meaning fewer mishaps and collisions. (The mountain's overall steepness helps too, according to Mr. Nelson. As he puts it, "When skiers fall down on

Locals' Lingo:

Ever sat on the Thunder chair or Sublette quad at Jackson Hole and listened to a local beside you raving about the powder in No-No Chute or Lonnie's Chute? Later, poring over your trail map, you couldn't find those trail names anywhere. Such runs are part of the vast underground lexicon of Jackson Hole.

If a chute, hanging snowfield, or slot between the trees has been skied, it's been named. As have many large rocks and several distinctive trees. The list of named landmarks is endless, and there simply isn't enough room on the trail map to pinpoint them all.

Most of these names were bestowed by the ski patrol, who use them to relay directions to accidents or to share information about slides started during avalanche control. Locals who heard them have appropriated the names for their own use, but few ski bums know the history behind them.

No-No Chute, for instance, was unintentionally named by resort founder Paul McCollister, who watched from a distance as two patrollers dropped into the narrow gully that plunges into Bernie's Bowl. Thinking the bottom of the gully too rocky to be safely skied, McCollister called out, "No! No!"and the name stuck.

Crabtree Rock, near the Après Vous lift, was named for Jeff Crabtree, owner of the equipment shop Skinny Skis and former mayor of Jackson. In 1966, the first year the resort was fully open, he hit

WHAT'S IN A NAME?

Williams in an avalanche early one morning while he and Kent Hoopingarner were doing snow control. The slope fractured between the two men; Williams, on the downhill side, grabbed for Hoopingarner's leg as the snow began to slide. Hoopingarner said, "Oh, no, you don't," and Williams went for a short, bumpy, and, fortunately, noninjurious ride, though he was pitched over fifteen-foot-high Diagonal Rock on the way down. Hoopingarner, as assistant patrol leader, immediately closed the mountain due to the dangerous conditions, and all the patrollers repaired to the Alpenhof to drink to Williams' luck.

One of the best stories tells of naming Lonnie's Chute, just below Tensleep Bowl and south of Downhill Chute. It was 1967, the tram had just recently opened, and Lonnie Ball was the only patroller at the top of Rendezvous when a volunteer member of the National Ski Patrol reported an accident in Tensleep Bowl. With the help of assistant snow ranger Rod Newcomb, Ball brought a toboggan to the scene, finding a skier with a dislocated hip.

"He was in a lot of pain," recalls Ball. "We couldn't even touch this guy. Rod pulls out a hypo needle, and that was the first I learned he was a paramedic. He gives this guy a shot, and I'm impressed, the national patrolman is impressed, and the guy immediately relaxes, says, 'Ha, I'm all right.' So we package him up, put all his ski equipment in the toboggan, and we talk about how to take him down. Instead

Lonnie Ball

the huge rock at full speed, breaking both legs above the ankles.

What most skiers know as Bivouac, patrollers call Wally World. In the old days, the entire south face of Cheyenne Bowl was gladed, making it Mark "Big Wally" Wolling's favorite powder stash. To make the terrain easier for intermediate skiers, however, the resort cut a swath through the face a number of years ago. Big Wally's somewhat sarcastic response was, "Wally World's not a place. It's a state of mind, where the fun never stops and all your dreams come true."

If a patroller's name is affixed to a chute or a steep face, it usually means he was caught in an avalanche there, as happened to former patrol leader Dean Moore in Dean's Slide, on the left side of Rendezvous Bowl. When it slid again in 1986, Dean's Slide killed Paul Driscoll. Silky's Slide, on the far side of the cirque, is named for another patrol leader, Bob "Silky" Sealander.

Kirby's Slide, just east of Tower Three Chute, caught Kirby

of taking the Downhill Chute, I thought we could go down this thing [the as-yet-unnamed gully] diagonally.

"Rod thought it sounded like a pretty good idea. So we head down, and the minute we break over [the lip of the chute], Rod's skis go out from underneath him, pulling me around backwards. I hang on as long as I can, bouncing, you know, and next thing I know I've lost the toboggan, too. There it goes. If it hadn't been for a bunch of little trees it hit, it probably would have gone all the way to the bottom.

"I still have my skis on, so I spin around and get up, and the national ski patrol guy, he's going crazy, of course. I go down there and the guy is completely out of the toboggan, his skis, everything, the whole package is out of the toboggan. I thought, 'He's dead, he's dead for sure.' And I open up the cover and the guy looks up at me and says, 'Are we at the bottom?'

"So I cover him back up, and Rod skis down to us. By then, I wanted one of those shots, too."

S'n'S Couloir:
A SHARED LEAP OF FAITH

S'n'S Couloir is Corbet's Couloir's mean, underfed little brother. About fifty yards south of Corbet's, S'n'S is a narrow gash in the golden rock of Rendezvous Mountain's upper tier. Ending in a smear of snow that funnels into Tensleep Bowl, the chute, like Corbet's, is visible from the aerial tram. But the tram's passengers, as they sail to Rendezvous's summit, rarely see a lineup of skiers atop S'n'S like they do above Corbet's. S'n'S intimidates all but the bravest or most oblivious.

Now, about that name. It stands for Simms and Sands, though not necessarily in that order. On a fine spring day in the early 1970s, while working as Jackson Hole ski patrollers, John Simms and Charlie Sands snuck away and leaped into the couloir. First, however, they made a pact never to tell who dropped in first. It still stands. But Simms, who'd been patrol director at Colorado's Arapahoe Basin before coming to Jackson, and Sands, who landed on patrol after his first winter in Jackson Hole as a dishwasher, are only too happy to tell the rest of the story. Here it is, in their words:

SIMMS: I remember it was a beautiful day, probably in March, and we'd just gotten some new snow. I just said to Charlie, "Let's go do something special."

SANDS: We'd talked about it on various tram rides. When Simms said, "Hey Charlie, let's go," I said, "Shit, okay."

SIMMS: We hooked our poles together and dangled them over the edge. Even our four poles hooked together didn't reach the snow, so we knew it was at least 16 feet. It's an elevator shaft— you look into it and you can't tell how deep it is.

SANDS: My biggest concern that day was the avalanche danger. Another concern was whether we were going to slam into the wall.

SIMMS: We probably stood there a half hour. One of us would go to the edge, look down, get ready, then say, "No, I lost it," and back off. Then the other would go to the edge.

SANDS: I told somebody, when they asked how I did S'n'S, that it was one of those days when

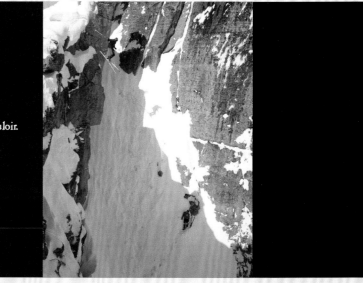

Ron Miller drops into S'n'S Couloir.

I had a bad hangover and I leaned over the edge and fell in. I wasn't an air guy. Shit, I remember thinking, when am I going to land? But it was a nice soft landing.

SIMMS: There's so much adrenaline after you do something like that.

SANDS: The biggest stir was going back up to the patrol room and pimping those guys.

SIMMS: We said, "You know that chute that's never been skied? We just did it."

SANDS: They all rushed out the door, put their skis on, and skied down to it. "We're proud of you, Charlie," they said. "You really did it."

SIMMS: We did agree, before we went in the couloir, not to say who went first.

SANDS: I've never told anybody, not even my wife. I don't think John has either. Even in my drinking days, people would ask me who went in first—you know, they'd set me up—and I'd never tell. And I've been asked a lot.

SIMMS: One of the big clothing companies—maybe The North Face—even made an S'n'S jacket.

SANDS: I think in those days [photographer] Bruce Morley had made an S'n'S poster. I was in the Moose one time, and this kid walks up to me, says, "Are you Charlie Sands?" I said, "Yeah." He says, "Will you sign this poster for me?" I felt like Ted Williams or Mickey Mantle. "Yeah, kid, I'll sign it," I said. "How many more do you want me to sign?"

Patroller Callum MacKay tosses a charge off the side of Rendezvous Mountain
as the sun rises over the Gros Ventre range.

the flats, they tend to splat more.") But as improved ski equipment allows less adept skiers to tackle more dangerous terrain and the resort more heavily markets itself to families, patrollers will surely be responding to more wrecks. Already on mornings without avalanche control, patrollers train rigorously for cliff rescues, avalanches, lift evacuations, and medical accidents. They're also providing more "courtesy rides" to customers who decide they can't get down the mountain on their own and would rather be brought down in a toboggan.

The patrollers themselves are changing, too. Of the fifty-six on staff, eight are women, double the number from just four years ago and a far cry from the early days when patrollers were only men. And though it's still considered the most difficult place in the country to land a patrol job, Corky Ward has lately augmented his crew with patrollers in their late twenties and early thirties, such as Kevin Brazell, Allison Bergh, Hollis Brooks, Mike Werner, Matt Kelly, Rod Newcomb's son Mark, and Jenna Malone, all of whom have lent the patrol a more youthful image.

But don't be too quick to count out the veterans. Asked when he'll retire, Mr. Nelson says, "Next year. But I've said that for

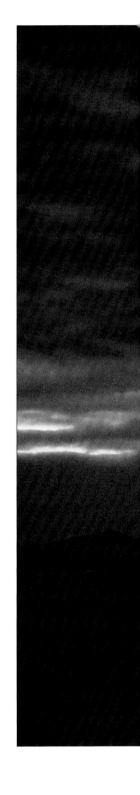

the last five years. I'm glad they don't try to squeeze us older people out."

They're too valuable to be squeezed out, affirms Ward. The patrol's oldest member is sixty-five-year-old Jerry Balint, whom Ward describes as, "a boss's nightmare. He's a prankster. He's got the world by the tail. But that keeps the stress in check. And when things go bad, when I need somebody very professional who has total grasp of rescues, he's one of the first people I look to."

In his trademark purple silk scarf and handlebar mustache, Balint looks like a Wyoming cowboy who's just stepped from his Tony Lama boots into a pair of Langes. Nicknamed "Cool Breeze" by his fellow workers, who like to say he's an eighteen-year-old in a sixty-five-year-old body, Balint embodies the ageless, smooth-talking, hard-bitten image of the Jackson Hole Ski Patrol. He's been patrolling for a quarter century, he's glad to tell you, and doesn't plan on leaving his mountain anytime soon.

"It's all here," he says, surveying his domain from the rim of Cheyenne Bowl. "Snow, work, skiing, weather. Pretty exciting place to work. I couldn't imagine doing anything else." ✳

Facing page: Mike Hattrup on the Crags. Left: Jerry Balint. Above: A benefit of being a patroller—sunrises and sunsets viewed from on high.

chapter 6

THE CREATION OF AN IMAGE

It's only 8:30 in the morning, but things are already getting hectic atop Rendezvous Mountain. The problem is the weather, which is clear and windless after two weeks of storms. On such mornings, when the long-awaited sun finally breaks over a horizon of untouched snow, each bowl, cliff, and ridge in the Tetons holds pictorial promise. Like moths to the light, every ski photographer and filmmaker in the vicinity converges on Jackson Hole Mountain Resort to make the images that will pay the rent for the rest of the year.

Accordingly, the 8:12 A.M. tram, reserved for such purposes, is packed with photographers. Among them is Wade McKoy, at forty-nine years old the platoon leader of local ski shooters. Joining Wade is a crew of filmmakers and skiers from Teton Gravity Research, the local band of erstwhile ski bums who've turned a clever name, slick logo, and some of the most hair-raising ski footage ever shot into a million-dollar empire. Likewise weighed down by backpacks full of steel, glass, and celluloid are local photographers Jonathan Selkowitz, Chris Figenshau, John Layshock, a British video crew, and a French photographer named François, each with his own brood of ski models.

Spirits are high. This is Jackson Hole, after all, where the photogenic terrain is endless and the aerial tram gets you there while the sun is still low. For ski shooters, there may be no more fertile hunting grounds on this continent. From the tones of their greetings to each other as the tram glides to its apex, it is apparent the photographers on board know they have it good.

But today's camaraderie on the tram devolves into chaos on the summit, at least for McKoy and TGR cinematographer Todd Jones, who often work together. Before the ski patrol gives the okay to do so, most of the models and photographers, including McKoy, scoot across the top of Rendezvous and out a backcountry gate. But Jones, checking in with patrol, is held back because a snowcat is still on the mountain, finishing up the previous night's grooming near the bottom. The lower mountain is worlds away from the hanging faces, cliffbands, and couloirs that are TGR's stock in trade, and Jones is irritated that the patrol won't let him follow his athletes across Rendezvous's crest. As he would say later, "I don't think [the patrollers] really get our program."

With Jones missing and the sun rising higher—flattening the light and baking

All in a day's work: Todd Jones films, Jason Prigge flies.

the snow—confusion ensues to a soundtrack of crackling walkie-talkies. Calling the situation, among more descriptive terms, a "train wreck," McKoy can do little more than wait on the high, windy shoulder of Cody Peak, the film crew's preordained meeting place.

Fortunately, word soon comes that Jones is on his way. Laboring under the weight of an Arriflex 16-millimeter camera, lenses, filters, and film—all stuffed into a thickly padded, custom-made backpack—Jones trudges up to McKoy's side to catch his breath and survey the scene. Also waiting atop Cody are professional skiers and snowboarders Rick Armstrong, Jason Tattersall, Micah Black, and Adam Hostetter, all household names to TGR's fans. Lining the brink of a snow-plastered gully, the

athletes point their ski poles at the cliff opposite, debating the photographic potential of two narrow spines that drop precipitously to the basin below. McKoy hands his Canon EOS camera and six hundred-millimeter lens to Tattersall, who wants to scope a line on the far spine.

"I'll ski in from just under the cornice," Tattersall announces, camera glued to his eye, "make a left turn on the upper section, facing you, drop the first rock, then make a right turn, away from you, and drop the

Left and left below: TGR cinematographers in their office—the Jackson Hole backcountry. Below: TGR talent and crew congregate on the shoulder of Cody Peak. Right: Micah Black on Pucker Face, Cody Peak.

second." He sounds like he's describing a few casual dance moves, albeit on a dance floor that is about two miles above sea level and a few degrees shy of vertical.

"Great," says McKoy.

Tattersall moves into position. Jones and McKoy, their tripods side by side, put their eyes to their viewfinders. Somebody starts a countdown, which echoes metallically from every walkie-talkie: "Five, four, three, two, one . . ."

Briefly hidden behind the spine, Tattersall scoots into view, crouching under the drooping wind lip at Cody's brow. Then, just as planned, he makes one left turn, spurts off the first rock, swoops right, and sails off the lower rock, launching for God-knows-how-many feet into the cirque below Cody. The clifftop erupts into howls.

"Ha, ha, the train wreck is over," McKoy enthuses.

The train, in fact, is just gathering steam, as "the boys" (as they call themselves) embark on their customary game of one-upmanship. Tattersall is followed by Hostetter, then by Armstrong. Finally Micah Black, who has been in every TGR flick since the first, 1996's *Continuum*, and bears the nickname Viper ("Because when he stays at your place, he'll vipe all the milk out of the fridge," laughs TGR's production assistant Todd

Above: TGR cofounder Corey Gavitt skis the "sticks" (tripod) back to the bottom. Right: Todd Jones.

Johnson) steps up, drops in, and launches the farthest into the bowl. As he sinks into the snow, his momentum hurls him back into the air and flips him forward twice, head over heels, leaving a line of craters in the slope like a skipping stone leaves dimples in water. When Black finally comes to a stop, buried hip deep in powder, he raises two snow-encrusted arms over his head in victory.

"Damn, Vipe'," mutters Jones, clearly pleased at the morning's turn of events, "you didn't have to go *that* big."

Bigness is what has always lured photographers and filmmakers to Jackson Hole. Whether shot from their flanks or from afar, the Tetons fill the frame. First to succumb to their visual siren song was William Henry Jackson, photographer for the Hayden Survey of 1872. Leading a heavily laden mule to the top of Table Mountain on the west side of the range, Jackson erected a portable darkroom on the summit so he could expose wet-plate negatives of the South, Middle, and Grand Tetons.

His impressively sharp images inspired a stampede of photographers that continues to this day. Who can blame them? The Tetons, as Teddy Roosevelt said, look like mountains should look and, therefore, beckon to every

Right: William Henry Jackson's 1872 view of the east side of the Tetons. Below: Carl Oksanen's 1999 view of the range's east side. The limber pine in the foreground, which stands on the sagebrush flats of Grand Teton National Park, is known as the "Old Patriarch."

camera that comes within range, whether it's arrived on the dashboard of a Winnebago, in a skier's backpack, or in a Hollywood studio's tractor trailer.

Since the 1920s, Hollywood has been besotted with the Teton Range. The mountains served as the flickering backdrop in two early silent films: 1921's *Nanette of the North* and 1922's *The Cowboy and the Lady.* In 1930 Jackson Hole welcomed its first major star, or, more accurately, star to be. The film was *The*

Big Trail; the first-time actor, a former studio prop man, was John Wayne.

In 1953 Paramount Studios chose the Teton Valley Ranch, the Elk Refuge, and Grand Teton National Park as locations for the classic western *Shane,* starring Alan Ladd. Henry Fonda came in 1960 to star in *Spencer's Mountain*; Clint Eastwood came in 1980 to film *Any Which Way You Can*; and Sylvester Stallone arrived in 1985 to direct the stirring "training in Siberia" scenes for *Rocky IV.*

Mostly these productions stayed on the valley floor. But in 1969, with the Jackson Hole ski resort recently opened, United Artists rose to the occasion, so to speak, filming *Mrs. Pollifax—Spy* atop Rendezvous Mountain. Starring Rosalind Russell, the movie is the somewhat implausi-

A Tale of Two Skids

Ski bumming isn't what it used to be. Scarce housing, an exorbitant cost of living, and one of the highest season-pass prices in the country make the classic ski-to-live, live-to-ski lifestyle a formidable challenge in Jackson Hole. Even those who escape the season-pass blues by working at the resort must work one or two additional jobs to pay for groceries and rent, leaving their ski time as skimpy as their paychecks. The attrition rate is high, with most postcollege ski bums giving up after a season or two.

But there are many in Jackson Hole who persist. For these stalwarts, skiing is not a hobby and the lifestyle is not negotiable. They make it work—however odious that word may be—in one of two ways: Either, after several years of strategizing, scrounging, and schmoozing, you land one of the valley's rare jobs with good pay and flexible hours, latch onto a place to live with minimal rent, and work out enough deals each year to keep yourself in new, or at least tuned, skis. Or you live in a cardboard box.

Which is how Mike Tierney, twenty-four, survived the 2000-01 ski season. His box was inside the Igneous ski factory, where he worked as a graphic designer. "I had a pretty sweet cardboard box, tucked into a corner of the shop," says Tierney. "I think a car came in it—it said Mazda on the side. It was kind of a shrine to skiers—there were pictures of all my friends on the walls."

Tierney's friends are his fellow competitors on the freeskiing circuit, many of whom have landed multiple sponsorship deals and magazine covers. Joining them on the competition podiums and in the pages of *Freeze*

Says fellow local Steve Haas, "Mike's way off the deep end. Mike does things that just amaze me. But he's a big-air guy. I'm not. I'm a skier."

That would be an understatement. Haas, forty, takes the term "ski bum" to an exalted level. For seven seasons in a row, he skied every month of the year. One season he skied 140 days without a day off. Knee surgery last year, however, has slowed him down a bit. "Now I take two days off a month," he says.

What makes Haas's enviable winter schedule possible is a dump truck. He drives one "fifty, sixty, sometimes seventy hours a week" during the summer and fall for a local construction company. The job, which lasts from May 1 to Thanksgiving, pays well enough that Haas hasn't worked during the winter since the mid-1980s. It also helps that his rent is minimal and that he can rent out his spare room when his "cash flow isn't too good."

Haas rarely pays heed to cash flow, however, even though he graduated from college with a finance degree. Skiing is, always has been, and always will be his preoccupation.

"I just love to ski," he says. "I can have fun skiing the groomers. I can ski really nasty shit and have fun. I can have fun just puttin' around. Whatever's out there, I just make the

Mike Tierney

and *Skiing* magazines is Tierney's current engrossing goal. To reach that goal, he knows what he has to do: Ski. Constantly.

"Every day I don't ski—like if I had to work in the factory all day—I feel like I wasted the day," he says. "I didn't live that day."

Living, it seems, has everything to do with scaring oneself to death. Tierney has a ski style somewhere between inspired and suicidal—and the scars to go with it. (Once, in an emergency room, a doctor asked Tierney, "Where's your kneecap?" He replied, "I don't know, that's your job.") Though he's lived in Jackson only since 1997, he's quickly made a name for himself on the local ski scene. Tierney's most notable feat is the line on Cody Peak he skied in 1999 and named "Igneous Rocks," in honor of his employer. From the summit, he carved turns down Cody's exposed western face, then slipped into a virgin, hanging couloir. Exiting the chute meant making a blind, sixty-foot leap to the apron below.

"It's not the biggest air I've ever done," says Tierney, "but it's probably the scariest."

best of it, I just go with the flow."

Of course, it helps to live six miles from a ski mountain that never ceases to surprise. "I've been doing this a long time," Haas says, "and I go out there every day and there's still more places to go, different things to do, stuff I haven't hit yet. It's still out there, the best run. I'm always looking for it, because I know it's out there."

He's not the only one looking. Haas is just one of a pack of legendary Jackson Hole locals—Brian Rudder, Rusty Scott, and Lynda Hunt among them—who ski hard and fast on telemark gear, all day, every day, despite their ages being nearly twice that of locals like Mike Tierney.

"Most of the guys I ski with are older than me," says Haas, "and they ski better now and they're stronger than I've ever seen them. So I don't see much changing for myself. How do I feel about being a forty-year-old ski bum? I think it's just awesome. I can't wait to be a fifty-year-old ski bum."

Above: John Wayne as he appeared in *The Big Trail*. Left: Rosalind Russell and Darren McGavin, stars of *Mrs. Pollifax—Spy*, in the mountains of "Albania."

ble story of an American widow who finagles a CIA assignment, only to find herself held hostage in a castle high in the mountains of Albania. Gene Downer, who worked on the film, remembers that whenever Russell rode the aerial tram to work, she would cower on the floor in the middle of the car, held hostage by her fear of heights.

How like Hollywood, one might think, to substitute Jackson Hole for Albania or Siberia. But it's not just feature-film direc-

tors who've played fast and loose with the truth while shooting here. In fact, the long, venerable history of filmmaking and photography at Jackson Hole Mountain Resort began with cinematic subterfuge, perpetrated by two filmmakers who would rewrite ski filmmaking history.

In 1964 Colorado filmmaker Roger Brown proposed to Paul McCollister a promotional film about Jackson Hole's brand-new resort. McCollister agreed, under one condition. "Paul said he'd give me a contract to make the film if I hired a local cameraman to catch the powder when it fell," recalls Brown, who continues to run his production company, Summit Films, from his home in Gypsum, Colorado.

Brown knew just the man. In 1963 he had contributed money to

Corbet and His Couloir

There are steeper runs at Jackson Hole Mountain Resort. (Insomnia, the most southerly of the Expert Chutes, comes to mind.) And there are more intimidating runs, if one considers some of the chutes and rocky faces just beyond the resort's boundaries. But no ski run at Jackson Hole—or indeed on the entire continent—is as mythical as Corbet's Couloir.

Granted, myths are not always to be trusted, especially when they're only a few decades in the making. And Corbet's Couloir is simply a rocky chute, of which there are hundreds in the Tetons. But Corbet's, its entrance guarded by a cliff, is in full view of the aerial tram as it nears Rendezvous Mountain's summit. The chute, therefore, has tempted or terrified nearly every skier who's ever come to Jackson Hole, and its reputation has steadily spread.

But Corbet's legend goes far deeper. How the couloir got its name, and how it had its first descent, are stories of drama, humor, and tribulation. Corbet's Couloir deserves its mythical status, though for better reasons than many people know.

In 1963, while still in the early stages of planning Jackson Hole Ski Resort, Paul McCollister skinned up Rendezvous Mountain with Exum climbing guide Barry Corbet. ("Skinning" means climbing on skis with long strips affixed to the ski bases so the skier can slide his skis forward, uphill, without sliding back.) As McCollister and Corbet crossed Tensleep Bowl, just under Rendezvous's uppermost brow of cliffs, Corbet pointed

ered the strongest in the party, but fate conspired to keep him from Everest's summit. In the Khumbu Icefall, Corbet's close friend Jake Breitenbach, a fellow Exum guide and one of his McKinley partners, was hit by a falling serac (ice tower) and pitched into a crevasse, where he perished. Having lost his longtime climbing partner, Corbet concentrated instead on supporting Jim Whittaker, who became the first American atop Everest, and on fixing ropes for the expedition's route on the west ridge. With the expedition running low on time and oxygen canisters, Corbet chose to stay behind during Tom Hornbein's and Willi Unsoeld's famed first traverse of the world's highest mountain. After all, he was one of the younger members of the expedition and was "pretty sure I'd get another chance," he says.

Returning to Jackson, Corbet was contacted by Roger Brown, who needed a local cinematographer for a promotional film about the new resort.

"Barry and I filmed each other," remembers

Right: Barry Corbet as Teton guide. Far right: Barry Corbet as writer and editor.

at a deep, snowy cleft in the cliffs. "People will ski that," he said. "It will be a run."

McCollister was skeptical. Corbet, however, was well qualified to guess the bold direction skiing would take at Jackson Hole. A truly visionary skier and mountaineer, Corbet was one of four young American climbers—three of them Jackson Hole residents—to make the first ascent of the southwest rib of Alaska's Mt. McKinley in 1959. According to *Time* magazine, the ascent was "the greatest pioneering climb remaining in North America." And Barry Corbet, wrote climbing companion Pete Sinclair in *We Aspired*, was "the most powerful among us."

Back in Jackson, Corbet made the first ski descent of a major Teton peak in 1961, guiding two clients to the summit of Buck Mountain and skiing the steep, exposed, upper massif with his boots unbuckled.

After his prophetic ski trip with McCollister, Corbet traveled to Nepal as part of 1963's All American Everest Expedition. Again, he was consid-

Roger Brown, "because we didn't have any other skiers. When I was filming Barry, he tore a ligament his knee and got a blood clot that went to his lungs. He had an embolism; it collapsed one of his lungs. Within a few months after he got out of the hospital, he went down to Antarctica and he climbed three of the four highest peaks there, including the Vinson Massif [the continent's highest]. It was extraordinary he could recover and do that. He's a super-human being."

While producing *Jackson Hole—Big Skiing*, Corbet and Brown became partners, and in 1967, began shooting their groundbreaking film, *Ski the Outer Limits*, which features two flips into Corbet's Couloir.

These flips, performed by Hermann Goellner and Tom Leroy in 1968, came only a year after the couloir's first unroped descent, by a nineteen-year-old ski patroller named Lonnie Ball. In the 1966-67 season, with the tram newly open, the accepted way to enter the couloir was to lower oneself in with ropes, and that was how Ball planned to make his own descent. His plans, however, quickly changed.

Explains Ball, who now lives in Bozeman, Montana, "One day I went down to Corbet's to rappell into it, had my ski tips over the edge of the cornice to take a look, and I felt the cornice collapse. There was nothing else to do—I pushed off, stuck the landing, and skied down. Right then, the tram went by. 'Oh no,' I thought, 'I'm going to lose my job.' Patrollers weren't supposed to do that stuff, especially alone. I denied it as long as I could."

Given that Corbet's presently bestows greater bragging rights than any other inbounds ski run in the country, Ball's denial is ironic. The patrollers who've succeeded him probably wish people still felt sheepish about dropping into Corbet's, but such is not the case for many skiers whose egos exceed their skills. Countless are the

Woodmency, son of local meteorologist Jim Woodmency, jumped into the couloir as an eight-year-old in 1997. Bartlett, who himself descended Corbet's at the age of nine, guesses Woodmency may not even be the youngest.

And yes, Corbet has skied the couloir. "I knew my kids were going to do it before I did," he says, "if I didn't get in there."

But Corbet would not ski it twice. Nor would he return to Everest to complete the climb he began in 1963. In May of 1968, while Corbet was shooting ski footage from a helicopter near Colorado's Pyramid Peak, the helicopter faltered and crashed. His back broken, Corbet was paralyzed from the waist down. It was a crushing blow to the man that Jeff Foott, a fellow Exum guide and one of Jackson Hole's earliest patrollers, called "an athlete beyond imagine."

In the wake of his accident, Corbet took over editing duties for Summit Films. The last film Brown and Corbet worked on together was 1974's *The Edge*, a full-length theatrical release about skiing, hang-gliding, climbing, and river-running. Subsequently, Corbet turned his attention to producing instructional and motivational films for fellow wheelchair users and those coping with paralysis, and writing *Options*, an "encyclopedia and bible" for the spinal-cord injured that is in its tenth printing. For nine years, he was the editor of *New Mobility Magazine*, and he has written several columns on disabilities for the *Denver Post*.

skiers and snowboarders who have ping-ponged down the chute. Picking up the pieces after such accidents, says patroller Tom Bartlett, can be grisly.

"We've had spiral fractures, broken jaws, head injuries, lots of stuff," says Bartlett, who has skied Corbet's nearly every day in his eleven winters as a patroller. "One guy from England wearing Big Feet (ski-boards) hurled himself off in really hard conditions. He broke both legs and his jaw and was knocked unconscious. And there was a visiting patrolman who broke his femur in Corbet's on the first run of his first day here."

There have been plenty of success stories as well. Skiers like "Sick" Rick Armstrong and Doug Coombs have leapt into the couloir from nearly every angle, even from the towering west wall. And Dean

Corbet, 64, is still, in many ways, a mountaineer, struggling among the crevasses of a society slow to grant rights to its less mobile members, and pushing for higher senses of self-respect and entitlement for the disabled.

He does, however, take an admittedly cynical view toward the naming of Jackson Hole's famed couloir. "It wasn't named until after my injury," says Corbet, "and I expect it was a sympathy vote. I really don't think there were a lot of other reasons to name it after me."

Corbet is mistaken. The couloir is aptly named, if only because the courage needed to push one's skis over the chute's lip is but the smallest token of courage that Corbet has needed since his climbing and skiing careers were wrenched away. Moreover, skiing his namesake couloir is a leap of faith, "a flight into space," as *Ski the Outer Limits* describes it. So has Corbet's life been since his accident, as he has hewed a path so that others in similar circumstances might follow.

Barry Corbet at work on *Ski the Outer Limits*,
his ski poles lashed to his pack.

the All American Everest Expedition, which put the first American, Jim Whittaker, on Everest's summit. One of the expedition members was Barry Corbet, Teton climbing guide and namesake for Jackson Hole's most famous couloir. Knowing the young mountaineer was interested in filmmaking, Brown brought Corbet on as a cinematographer and partner in Summit Films.

There was one more challenge to hurdle. A promotional film about Jackson Hole would be incomplete without the resort's flagship, the aerial tram. But the tram itself was incomplete. All that existed at the time was the spindly work tram, used to hoist construction materials to Rendezvous's summit. So McCollister constructed an imita-

tion tramcar of plywood, then mounted this fake shell onto the work tram. "That's what we shot," remembers Brown. "And it worked. Everybody who saw the film thought the tram was finished."

After its starring role, the fake tram was put to use as a lift ticket office, first at Teton Village and later in downtown Jackson, at the Pink Garter Plaza.

Named *Jackson Hole—Big Skiing*, the promo was Corbet's and Brown's first collaboration and the first big-screen celebration of

a Andrews, in an
e that became the
for Greg Stump's
License to Thrill.

Jackson Hole's larger-than-life image. Brown and Corbet followed it with *Yoohoo, I'm a Bird*, featuring Pepi Stiegler's soaring gelande jumps from a ramp near the top of Après Vous.

In 1967 and '68, Corbet and Brown produced a movie that completely shook up ski filmmaking, which until then had been dominated by John Jay's and Warren Miller's travelogues. From the moment *Ski the Outer Limits* opens with an artful montage of the French Alps, it's clearly of a different stripe. "Man looks

to the stars," the narrator solemnly recites. "Since the beginnings he has reshaped, redefined his environment... As man explores the edge of the impossible, he crosses a threshold to the outer limits."

The film then cuts to Jackson Hole and Hart Ski Team legend Tom Leroy swan diving in extreme slow motion from the unmistakable cusp of Corbet's Couloir. Tucking into a perfect front flip, he lands deep in the gully's throat.

"These, then, are the outer limits," the narrator intones, "a flight into space, reaching to regain a shadow. The forms are many and varied, the purpose is free expression and the declaration of new limits."

Patroller Joe Larrow claims his fame in the early film *Rhythms*.

From Corbet's the film cuts to ski racing (with a brief shot of a racer plunging down Jackson Hole's extraordinary former downhill course), then builds gradually to its most striking sequence: a slow motion montage of Tom Leroy, Roger Staub, and Herman Goellner flipping through the air with only blue sky behind, their 210-millimeter Hart skis nearly grazing the lens. All the while, the weighty narration continues, nearly to the point of self-parody. But the words were sincere, says Brown.

"*Ski the Outer Limits* was a spontaneous reaction to how we felt," he explains. "It was quite genuine. It took an overview and dug a little deeper into the real feelings of the sport. You know, that's when man was first getting to the moon, so the idea of pursuing the outer limits was in the minds of people."

The film continues to be lauded as visionary. In December 1999, *SKI* Magazine included Brown in its list of the "100 Most Influential Skiers," maintaining that the movie "created a new genre of on-the-edge skiing images, paving the way for a later generation of moviemakers and germinating the seed of extreme skiing."

The film, which concludes with Austrian Goellner's own flip into Corbet's, includes some extreme locations: If Jacksonites look closely, they'll notice a very brief shot of two skiers ripping up the thin ribbon of snow that collects on East Gros Ventre Butte, just above town. Now known as the Taco Bell Couloir, this chute can no longer be legally skied. At least in retrospect, *Outer Limits* even went off limits.

When Corbet's helicopter accident in 1968 left him partially paralyzed (see p. 120), he took over editing duties for Summit Films. Brown returned to Jackson Hole in 1969 to shoot much of *The Great Ski Chase*, which starred Fred Iselin, the Swiss-born "Clown Prince of Skiing" and Aspen Highlands ski school director. The plot is purposefully absurd: Iselin, who's stolen a load of Hart skis, pursues young lovelies while a posse of hot skiers pursues him across the slopes of Jackson Hole, Vail, Aspen, and Chamonix. Nevertheless, it includes even better ski footage than *Outer Limits*.

Particularly noteworthy are a quick shot of somebody skiing over Corbet's massive west wall and the sequence that begins with Iselin's pursuers lowering themselves from Jackson Hole's tram,

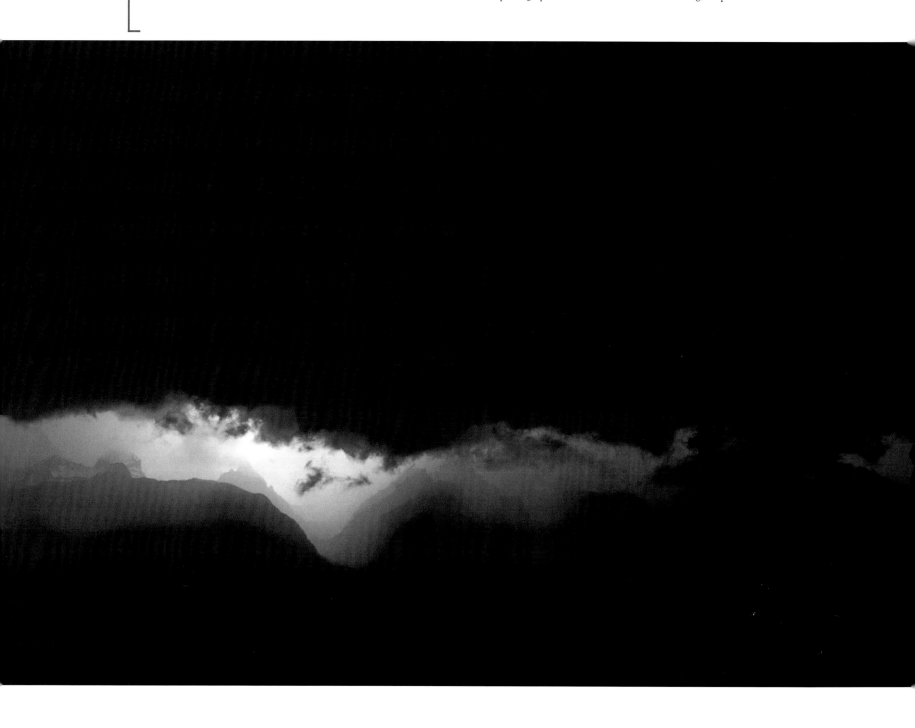

hundreds of feet above Tensleep Bowl. Dropping from the sky, the posse chases the leather-jacketed Iselin across Rendezvous Bowl and into Rock Springs Canyon. The action moves fast, and Brown filmed all of it while on skis himself.

"Those are the fastest travel shots I ever did," he recalls. "I must have been going sixty miles per hour."

Also not to be missed is long-legged Olympian Suzy Chaffee swinging down Amphitheater Run in a black cowboy hat and a bright orange, skintight ski suit. Iselin's character, recalls Brown, was a bit too lecherous for the sponsors' liking, but in this sequence, "the Romeo ski thief" can be excused for his attentiveness to Chaffee's ski form.

Though Pepi Stiegler had starred in a few promos and documentaries, it wasn't until the mid-1970s that other Jackson skiers made the big screen. Shot entirely at Jackson Hole and nearby Grand Targhee, *Rhythms* was a promotional film for Salomon ski boots, set to a jazz soundtrack. Producers Norman and Tyler Nelson used several local skiers, including Bill "Mad Dog" Danford, as talent, but it was a Jackson Hole ski patroller who stole the show.

Like *Ski the Outer Limits*, *Rhythms*

Above: A Bob Woodall self-portrait. Left: In the 1970s Frankie Bare flipped from the tram, a stunt performed for a European ski magazine. Below: Wade McKoy in the Jackson Hole backcountry.

begins and ends with an impressive leap into Corbet's. But this one was unplanned. Standing by in case the filmmakers had an emergency, Patroller Joe Larrow decided he deserved a place in the film. Corbet's, after all, was part of his morning snow control route. He announced his intentions to the skeptical film crew, then hiked all the way up to the patrol hut. Still-photographer Bob Woodall, who watched from a nearby buttress, remembers it well: "He skated and poled down the

hill to get as much speed as he could. He ducked the rope [strung across the couloir's lip] and popped it like a gelande. He flew so far, he flew right out of my frame."

The memory of Larrow in midair, the white crosses on his patrol jacket perfectly visible, is just as vivid for Norm Nelson: "Every camera had to adjust because no one expected a skier to appear that high in the frame. He screamed it really well, made a fabulous tumble, and came up with victory hands in the air. We freeze-framed it and used it to end the show."

Woodall remembers that McKoy, his business partner, went to Montana during the *Rhythms* shoot to photograph a solar eclipse.

Skier: Bissell Hazen.

Woodall almost went himself. "I can always find another total eclipse," says Woodall, "but I don't think I'll ever see [Larrow's jump] again."

Long the caretakers of Jackson Hole's proud photography tradition, Woodall and McKoy met while helping build the Casper chairlift in the summer of 1974. The year before, Woodall had heard that the Ski Corporation was dissatisfied with the photographer assigned to shoot the popular Nastar races. (These were the heady days of Nastar, when sponsor Schlitz Beer gave away samples at the races.) Sensing an opportunity, he installed a darkroom in a janitor's closet in the Sojourner Inn. Needing a partner, he asked McKoy to join him.

Until then, ski photographers struggled to forge careers in Jackson. Jim Elder, the resort's first official photographer, all but retired from ski photography when photos of snowmobiling proved more lucrative. Fletcher Manley, who freelanced extensively in the mid-1960s (his wife, Renee, "shot while giving a dazzling smile in Jackson Hole, Wyoming," got her own foldout page in the September 1969 issue of *SKI*), gave up after a few years and moved to San Francisco, though he returned intermittently to Jackson. "Jackson Hole was a hard place to cut it," says Manley,

Skier: A.J. Cargill

who now lives in New Hampshire. "It was so removed from the world."

Also attempting to make his livelihood by shooting skiing was Bruce Morley, son of resort cofounder Alex Morley. Though his relation to the resort afforded some interesting opportunities—he was Jackson Hole's first tram conductor in the summer of 1966 and the ski school's first alpine guide—it didn't make a photographic career any easier. Morley had some successes, shooting Franz

Klammer in the 1975 Wild West Classic, for example, and capturing local John Gonnella for the cover of *Playboy*'s 1975 ski calendar, but found the job frustratingly unprofitable. "You can't afford to do it for a living unless you're really good and really lucky," he told *Jackson Hole Magazine* in 1991.

McKoy and Woodall, however, have endured to make Focus Productions, their assignment/stock photography/publishing firm, a success. Certainly they're very good, but they've also made their own luck. Woodall landed a job as staff photographer for the *Jackson Hole Guide* in 1976, a position he held for ten years, and in 1978, McKoy wrote and photographed his breakthrough piece for *Powder* magazine,

"Craze Teaches Fool that Once Is Enough but Twice Is Nice," an adaptation of journal entries about Cody Peak's two famous couloirs. A lasting relationship between *Powder* and McKoy was forged, and thus was Jackson Hole's brand of high-stakes, out-of-bounds skiing introduced to the reading world.

"At that time, there were ten, possibly twenty people here who skied those kinds of lines," recalls McKoy. "There were some ski patrollers, a few ski schoolers, and some other mountain workers and ski bums. It was pretty radical stuff."

Nowadays, Cody's couloirs are skied on a daily basis, and there is no lack of local athletes willing to blast down them for

McKoy's and Woodall's cameras. Thanks to the right venue and vision, the Focus Production team helped create the "extreme" tsunami, then rode it to international renown. All the while, however, they've remained true to their roots as ski bums who taught themselves the exacting art of combining snow, skis, and slide film.

Appropriately, Focus Productions, Inc., World Headquarters (as the sign on the door proclaims) is less an office than a medieval-style catacomb occupied by two mad monks bent over

Left: James Malkmus on
No Name Peak.
Right: Mike Chambers
in the backcountry.

sheets of slides instead of illuminated manuscripts. You can't just walk through the office—you have to squeeze through file cabinets crammed with Woodall's and McKoy's work, stacks of magazines (likewise filled with their work), computers, ski gear, and light tables. A floor-to-ceiling fresco of posters, prints, and laser copies covers the walls, each one depicting a skier exploding through powder or arcing through the Wyoming sky.

Here, too, Woodall and McKoy have aided and advised an ever-growing group of protégés. As ski and snowboard magazines have proliferated, so have the photographers who've made Jackson Hole their career launching pad. Today at least ten local photographers make a living shooting skiing and other mountain sports, including Jonathan Selkowitz, Chris Figenshau, John Layshock, Greg Von Doersten, Jeff Diener, Florence McCall, Greg Epstein, and Andrew McGarry. Few are the outdoor magazines and catalogues that don't include some of these names in their photo credits.

Some of McKoy's and Woodall's ski models have also made good. When Teton Gravity Research flashed onto the scene in 1996, it had been almost thirty years since any Jackson locals had made

serious inroads into the ski film industry. Certainly the Tetons had been on several filmmakers' itineraries in the interim. In 1979, for example, Dick Barrymore had invited a young Greg Stump to Jackson to ski for his cameras; a decade later, Stump returned to shoot part of *License to Thrill*. But no modern ski filmmakers had thought to make Jackson a home base until locals Todd Jones, Steve Jones, Dirk Collins, and Corey Gavitt decided to try their hand at what they perceived as a stagnating genre.

"Todd and I skied for other film companies, and it was a turn off," says Steve Jones, who's two years older than brother Todd. "They'd come all the way here to film us and then not want to walk over to the good stuff."

Adds Collins, "We were bummed out you never got to see a skier's whole line, we were bummed out by the music they used—there were a lot of things we didn't think were being done right. So we sat down and decided we were going to show skiing the way we wanted to see it."

This meant teaching themselves how to shoot it. After a summer of commercial fishing in Alaska, each of the four partners pitched in three or four thousand dollars to buy cameras and film. At first, remembers Steve Jones, all the

film they shot came back "marginal." Then, over two days in the Teton backcountry, everything came together. "All of us were shooting and skiing, trading cameras, when Todd dropped in to a line above a cliff—I think it was a fifty-footer—and the thing just circled him, cracked all around him, and washed him over the cliff band," says Jones. "I mean, he just got sucked over, and I watched the whole thing from a stone's throw away. I remember saying to Dirk, 'Did you keep shooting that?' Dirk said,

'Yeah I kept shooting it.' Dirk couldn't have nailed it more, and the rest of the day was just as insane. Todd would be shooting, then he'd see something he wanted to ski. He'd be like, 'Hey, Dirk, can you shoot this for a second? And he'd go drop an eighty-footer, and everybody would be hyped. The energy would be contagious. He'd go back and go, 'Okay, who's up next?'"

Collins says, "That's when TGR became a film company. The film came back [from the processing lab], and we'd finally figured it out—everything came back perfect. When we hardly knew how to put film in the camera, that was a pretty big feat."

The harvest from those two days became one of the climactic

sequences of *Continuum*, TGR's inaugural production. The ski world, particularly the hometown audience, immediately embraced this brash new style of ski flick. Before the film's editing was even finished, the phone at the Jones brothers' house began ringing with orders. At the film's premiere, at Teton Village's Walk Festival Hall, the filmmakers expected a few hundred people; looking outside before the show, they were stunned to find a line of locals stretching all the way through Teton Village to the parking lot.

Collins laughs at the memory: "There was a line of cars coming down the village road, like that movie *Field of Dreams*—'If you build it they'll come.'"

And they keep coming. Since then, Teton Gravity Research has offered its adrenaline-addicted audience nine more films, including a whitewater kayaking movie, a surfing movie, and another hour-long ode to big mountain skiing and snowboarding, *Mind the Addiction*. With video cassette sales, stock footage sales, a clothing line, and a sprawling office at the base of Jackson Hole Mountain Resort, TGR is a veritable cottage industry. Meanwhile, the founders try to keep their

Far left: Owen Black threads the needle in S'n'S Couloir. Left: The Beaver Creek fire in 1985 burned much of the glacial moraines below the Grand Teton. The denuded pine trunks have become a stark visual element well appreciated by photographers.

heads above water in a business nearly growing out of control.

"It's overwhelming at times," says Steve Jones. "We thought we were going to be commercial fishing every summer and just working on the films in the winter. But it's 365 [days a year] now."

In the mountains, the TGR team has impeccable control. Deep in Alaska's Chugach range, a favorite stomping ground, TGR's cameras have recorded Jeremy Jones (Todd and Steve's younger brother), Jeremy Nobis, Gordy Peifer, Micah Black, and others screaming down entire mountainsides in ten, three, sometimes no turns, or skipping from spine to spine on sixty-degree, fluted faces as if they were cruising intermediate bump runs on Après Vous. In Jackson Hole, the crew spends several months each winter seeking out cliffs and couloirs in the backcountry that nobody before thought skiable.

It seems the greatest danger TGR faces is its own success. As audience and output increase, the young filmmakers' purist approach to ski films—high-octane skiing set to high-octane music, with few interruptions—risks becoming formulaic. But just as Roger

Above: Steve Jones, Dirk Collins, and Todd Jones in their Teton Village editing suite. Right: Chris Collins flips for TGR's cameras.

Brown believed in the philosophical message of *Ski the Outer Limits*, these inheritors of Jackson Hole's cinematic tradition—who are themselves probing Brown's and Corbet's notion that "today's absolute limit is tomorrow's commonplace"—believe wholeheartedly in their own vision.

"Sure, we could do things just to be different," says Steve Jones, "but most of the people in our market don't want to see skits, they just want to see the sickest things that happen each year in skiing. That's what we produce."

It helps that many of these "sickest things" happen in TGR's own backyard, on the mountain that looms directly beyond the office windows. TGR's films inspire Jackson Hole's already motivated locals to push their own limits further, which in turn inspires the filmmakers to distill that spirit on celluloid. Life imitates art, and the artists scramble to keep up. If, indeed, its films are formulaic, Teton Gravity Research hopes this is the formula the audience comes away with.

As Collins says, "This isn't something we made up in a boardroom—it's something we live every day."

Like many snowboarders who grew up in the valley, Kingwill learned to board on Snow King, occasionally cutting class to ride powder at Jackson Hole Mountain Resort. "That was a treat," he says, "to ski the big mountain." The first year he snowboarded seriously, as a thirteen-year-old, he competed in a halfpipe competition at Teton Village and took third place, though most of his competitors were professionals. These days Kingwill is also one of the most successful halfpipe competitors in the country: He's taken first place at several FIS World Cup competitions, snagged the Grand Prix Halfpipe Championship in 2000, and stood on countless podiums here and abroad. But what he truly wants is an Olympic medal in 2002.

"There are a lot of professional snowboarders out there riding in films and acting cool," says Kingwill. "I want to be different. In fifty years, I want to look back and tell my kids I went to the Olympics."

Kingwill isn't the only Jackson Hole snowboarder who's had Olympic aspirations. In 1998, Julie Zell hoped to qualify for the U.S. Olympic snowboard team as a GS racer. She ended up, she says, "Sixth or seventh nationally, and they took four athletes to Nagano." But if Zell has one overriding characteristic, it's resilience. She may, in fact, be Jackson Hole's most versatile snowboarder, having proven herself on the race course, on the big mountains of Alaska, and most recently, in boardercross events. In 2001, she finished the boardercross tour in second place in the U.S. and tenth in the world. And this surely won't be the last snowboarding challenge Zell meets. "I'm kind of ready to move into something new," she says, "but when I'm out there on the mountain, I'm not ready to move on at all."

For Stephen Koch, a snowboarding apprenticeship at Jackson Hole led not into manmade halfpipes but onto the summits of the world's highest mountains. In 2002, if things go as planned, Koch will become the first per-

Jackson Hole's Snowboarders Go Big

Julie Zell

First came San Diego surfer Mike Doyle, who arrived in 1972 to test and promote his invention: the monoski. His board gained a small local following, and throughout the 1970s the occasional monoskier was seen at the ski resort, on Cody Peak, or on Teton Pass.

But traversing across a slope on a monoski is excruciating, and today the boards have few adherents. By the early Eighties, however, surfing the Tetons, Doyle's original dream, had become a reality. Today, snowboarders are every bit as important as skiers on the Jackson scene. As snowboarding has diversified, Jackson Hole's riders have slid into influential positions in every niche, proving yet again that there are no better training grounds for the professional winter athlete.

If success could be measured by the grandiosity of one's appearance, then Rob Kingwill would, indeed, be king. Twice his image has appeared on giant billboards in San Francisco, the result of his sponsorship by Nike. "Michael Jordan, Renaldo [the Brazilian soccer star], and I are the only ones to get two billboards," he says. "And I'm just a snowboard kid from Jackson."

son to have snowboarded the Seven Summits, the highest peaks on all seven continents. Only Mount Everest stands in his way." That's the ultimate," he says. "There's a line I'd like to do that hasn't been skied yet. It's about nine thousand or ten thousand feet long, with a consistent pitch of forty degrees."

No doubt he'll be up to the test. After learning to snowboard at Jackson Hole in 1987, he made the first snowboard descent of the Grand Teton only two years later. Thus began Koch's onslaught of the Tetons, which has included unrepeated descents of Nez Perce's Spooky Face and the Grand Teton's Black Ice Couloir, which is as nefarious as it sounds.

Today, Koch climbs and rides his board around the world but still spends much of his year in Jackson Hole, as an Exum climbing guide in the summer and an alpine guide at Jackson Hole Mountain Resort in the winter. Even with Everest looming large on the horizon, Jackson Hole is still his preferred training ground. "I don't need higher altitude training than what we have here," he says. "It's inspiring here. This place makes me want to get out into the hills. I don't really look at it as training. It's just fun."

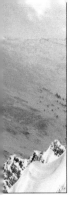

chapter 7

THE WILD BEYOND

Just south of Rendezvous Mountain is a broad, craggy promontory, a viking helmet without horns. This is Cody Peak (officially named Peak 10,753, for its elevation in feet), the former venue for the National Powder 8s competition and a frequent backdrop for the photos splashed across Jackson Hole's trail maps and brochures.

But Cody isn't just a gleaming abstraction behind a ski model's spray of snow. Beyond the ski area's boundaries, and therefore off-limits to skiers for most of the resort's history, Cody's upper massif has long embodied freedom, boldness, and the urge to write solitary tracks on the most visible location possible. Cody compels every passenger on the Sublette quad or the tram to study its striking contours, hanging snowfields, and deep clefts, none of which, to the unaccustomed eye, seem skiable.

But everything on Cody that holds snow has been skied. Between 1966 and 1999, skiers and snowboarders, driven by the promise of local glory, scouted, descended, and named at least nine different routes on the mountain. Some, like Four Shadows and No Shadows, are merely exhilarating. A few rank among the most extreme—no way to get around the word—ski routes in the Rockies.

Take Central Chute, for example. First skied by Larry Detrick and Steve Lundy in 1974, Central features consistent, do-or-die steepness, a massive cornice at the top, a narrow constriction in the middle, and a twenty- to fifty-foot cliff (depending on snow depth) at the bottom. Tales abound of skiers who, unnerved by the big-air exit, took their skis off and hiked back out of the chute.

On Cody's south side, invisible to chairlift passengers but no less exalted, are two lengthy chutes: Once Is Enough and Twice Is Nice. Who skied them first, probably in the mid-1970s, is arguable; what isn't debatable is what happens to the hair on the back of your neck when you stare down their throats. Several skiers have survived nasty falls in these couloirs. In 2001, ski coach Eric Rohr skied halfway down Twice to its dogleg, only to look up and watch his ski partner set off an avalanche. It hurtled toward Rohr and blasted him out of the couloir. He fell 350 feet, tumbling over rocks, near-vertical snow, and, finally, a twenty-foot cliff. When he landed in the snowfield below, Rohr checked himself over, dusted himself off, and went to ski No Name Face.

Such stories have become almost commonplace. Formerly, skiers waited until late

Though Cody Peak is barely one and a half miles from the top of Jackson Hole's aerial tram, its harrowing couloirs and hanging faces are worlds away from the resort. Here, James Malkmus makes a precarious entrance into the steepest side of Once is Enough.

In March, 1995, snowboarder Stephen Koch pioneered a new line on Cody Peak he called "Talk is Cheap." He descended the Hanging Snowfield directly below the summit and then rappelled into Central Chute, the dark gully in the center of the photo.

spring, when snow is usually more stable, to climb Cody's north ridge and attain its steep couloirs. Now, whenever there is adequate snow in Once, Twice, and Central, tracks snake down their rock-lined gullets. Four Shadows, No Shadows, and the aptly named Pucker Face all see steady traffic.

Why the change? Certainly Jackson Hole skiers are more skilled and gutsier than ever. And current high-performance backcountry ski equipment allows more skiers to tackle previously unapproachable terrain. But something else is going on, too—a loosening of the old rules, a fresh impetus to explore, an unprecedented nonchalance. All you have to do is look toward Cody, and to the fresh web of tracks in the wake of each storm, to realize a new age is upon Jackson Hole.

In 1999, Jackson Hole Mountain Resort made a long-awaited policy change: Skiers henceforth would have full-time access to the peaks and canyons beyond the resort's orange boundary signs. Formerly, the entry gates to this sought-after terrain were opened only when the ski patrol deemed avalanche danger to be low, usually just a few days before the resort closed in April. But this made the ski area potentially liable for any skier injuries or fatalities in the backcountry. And it was debatable

While most skiers are still fast asleep dreaming of powder, Bob Comey is hard at work measuring it.

As the Bridger-Teton National Forest avalanche forecaster, Comey uses a battery of instruments on Rendezvous Mountain to measure the snowfall, its moisture content, wind direction and speed, temperature, and barometric pressure. With these measurements and some help from the National Weather Service, he can assess the avalanche danger at Jackson Hole Mountain Resort and in the surrounding backcountry, advise the ski patrol and the public about it, and take a calculated guess at what the weather will bring next. All before 8 A.M.

To get to Comey's office, the Bridger-Teton Forest Avalanche Lab, you must walk through the innards of the tram dock in Teton Village, past the huge engines and bullwheel, and climb the stairs to a long, narrow room crammed with computers, fax machines, maps, and file cabinets full of historical weather data. At the far end a small window faces Rendezvous Mountain, which seems to hover just outside the room like a patient curious about the doctor's diagnosis.

Comey knows his patient's condition well. Scattered across the ski area are seven "study plots," clusters of instruments continuously recording the snowfall, temperature, and wind speed. (New snow is measured by sound beams that bounce off the snow's surface to a sensor. This method works well for all but the lightest snow, which explains why snow measurements may seem modest on frigid days.) In his office by

Early U.S. Forest Service snow ranger Juris Krisjanson consults a strip chart, showing wind speeds on Rendezvous Mountain, in the Bridger-Teton National Forest Avalanche Lab.

5:30 A.M., Comey downloads the study plots' data, then sends it to the National Weather Service office at Riverton. In less than a half an hour, the office replies with a forecast for the next eight hours. Included in the forecast is a summary, designated as RPK 1, 2, or 3. RPK 1 means that zero to three inches of snow are expected on Rendezvous Peak; RPK 2 translates into four to six inches; and RPK 3, a joyful indicator to local powderhounds, anticipates a snowfall of six inches and up.

Meanwhile, Comey listens to any avalanche or snowpack observations that have been offered by backcountry skiers on the lab's voicemail system and downloads satellite maps and regional forecasts. He then distills everything into the day's avalanche forecast, which he posts on the avalanche lab's website and records for the local avalanche report phone line. Finally, Comey, or assistant forecasters Jim Farmer or Jim Springer, prepare a detailed rap to give to the patrollers on the 8 A.M. tram ride.

Though it's a lot of work, most mornings, says Comey, "it's pretty casual. But if we get a lot of new snow, we've got more things to count, more things to think about. And the patrol goes up the hill earlier, at 7:30 A.M. So we have more to do and less time to do it in."

The lab workers aren't done, however, when the forecast is finished. Besides being employed by the Forest Service to produce the forecast, Comey and his assistants are also patrollers, responsible for their own snow control routes. This allows them to "get their feet in it," finding out for themselves what parts of the mountain are most dangerously loaded and where slabs have formed. Such firsthand observation is invaluable, observes Comey: "If you're headed for the backcountry, you can't just go out there blindly. You have to pay attention to what's going on around you. We just provide information—you make the decisions."

The avalanche lab's daily forecasts can be found at www.untracked.com/forecast or by calling 307-733-2664.

Left: James Malkmus leaves a lone signature on No Name Peak, south of the ski resort. Below: Patrollers post the day's avalanche conditions each morning at every backcountry access point.

CAUTION
YOU ARE LEAVING THE
JACKSON HOLE SKI AREA BOUNDARY
THIS IS YOUR DECISION POINT

whether the resort could actually control access to the adjacent Bridger-Teton National Forest and Grand Teton National Park.

With the change the resort placed the option to go O.B. squarely on the shoulders of its customers. No longer would the resort patrol the backcountry, do avalanche control beyond its boundaries, or assume liability for any backcountry accidents. If a skier chooses to venture through one of the six access gates strung along the resort's boundaries, it is his or her responsibility to know the ins and outs of backcountry travel and carry the requisite gear: an avalanche beacon, a shovel, a probe pole, and extra food, water, and clothing.

Such an "open-gate" policy was already in place at many U.S. ski

areas when Jackson Hole made its decision. As resort president Jerry Blann said at the time, "We're only coming into concert with what's happening in every other national forest across the country." But Jackson Hole's change of heart had additional implications. No other national forest contained a two-and-a-half-mile-long, 4,139-foot-high aerial tram disgorging passengers atop untold acres of avalanche-prone terrain.

Though the resort initially downplayed

Left: Tom Turiano leads the Ferrer family, from Connecticut, toward the top of Four Pines, a sparsely treed ridge south of the resort. Below: Earning their turns: skiers head up a ridge above the south fork of Granite Creek.

the decision, the skiing world did not. Every print and Internet publication having anything to do with skiing, from MountainZone.com to *Ski Area Management*, publicized the move, making much of the Tetons' wild topography and the new opportunity to indulge in European-style, lift-served, off-piste exploration.

But you'd be hard-pressed to find such a variety of skiable terrain in the Alps—from open glades to glacial cirques, gloomy canyons to wide plateaus—as you do in the Tetons. And nowhere in Europe or North America can you find such a combination of easy access, vertical relief, and deep, light snow. For a skier with the know-how, Jackson Hole's backyard is an incomparable playground.

Just ask Tom Turiano. Tall, rawboned, and soft-spoken, Tom published *Teton Skiing, A Guide and History* in 1995, after logging an estimated four thousand miles of ski tours through the range. Since then, he estimates that he's skied another two thousand miles in the Tetons, prodding his skis and leather telemark boots into nearly every drainage and onto more than a hundred summits north and south of the Jackson Hole ski resort. Currently writing another guidebook, *The Selected Peaks of Greater Yellowstone*, and guiding skiers beyond ski-area boundaries, Tom lives and breathes ski

Wild snow begets wild ideas. At least, that's the pattern at Jackson Hole, where ski patrollers and backcountry skiers have responded to the challenges of deep snow, severe terrain, and unpredictable weather by inventing a host of innovative tools and clothes.

If there's an inventor emeritus in Jackson Hole, it's John Simms, who, as he puts it, has "sort of a wild imagination." As a patroller and then a snow ranger at the ski resort in the early 1970s, he founded Snow Research Associates, which devised and sold snow study tools that avalanche forecasters around the world found invaluable. Then Simms devised a coupling device that allowed two poles, with their grips removed, to be screwed together. The result was a single, long, avalanche probe pole. The Life-Link, as he called it, took off immediately, first among Simm's fellow patrollers, then among backcountry adventurers. From its success sprang Simms' new company, Life-Link International, which also produced the first polycarbonate backcountry shovel and now manufactures a full line of backcountry products.

Simms is no longer in the gear business, having turned to large-scale metal sculpture. His gear inventor's torch has been passed to Russell Rainey, founder of Rainey Designs and maker of several revolutionary telemark ski bindings.

Rainey's first binding, devised in 1987, was a piece of stout rubber tubing attached to a metal toeplate. Living in Arkansas at the time, he hit the road and headed for the Rockies, selling about two-hundred pairs of his unique free-heel binding out of the back of his truck. Soon afterward,

uniform. Spend any time at the ski resort, on Teton Pass, or at Pearl Street Bagels, and you'll notice an abundance of stretchy jackets with two vertical pockets on the chest. Though the pockets have become Cloudveil's trademark, they're there for a reason: They're easy to reach with a backpack on, and they can be opened for ventilation.

On the strength of its sales, Cloudveil has widened its product mix to include ski pants, fleece jackets, T-shirts, shorts, hats, and gloves, all made with state-of-the-art materials. As Brian Cousins says, "Around here you learn pretty quickly that traditional outerwear doesn't cut it."

Jackson Hole's most famous outdoor-related product, however, was made of nothing so fancy as a shred of neoprene. In 1974, ski patroller Robbie Fuller and some friends had acquired some of the rubbery material to make kayak spray skirts. As Fuller recalls, "I needed something to hold my glasses up, so I cut a little piece out, rolled up the ends, and it worked." Thus was the ubiquitous "Croakie" born. Like John Simms' products, it was first snapped up by his fellow patrollers, and its popularity spread from there. "At first I traded them for beers," Fuller recalls. "The next winter my wife Zaidee and I started making lots of them, with tools instead of just scissors." After a few years and about 28,000

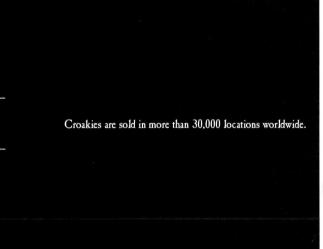

Croakies are sold in more than 30,000 locations worldwide.

he moved to Wilson, Wyoming, and became an Exum climbing guide. He spent winters skiing in the Tetons and tinkering in his workshop, and soon invented the first telemark binding to incorporate a compression spring. Its immediate successor, the famed SuperLoop, "got to be known as *the* performance tele binding," says Rainey.

In 2001, he released the HammerHead, "the synthesis of everything I learned in the past 15 years." It's a cunning device, with a heel-throw that looks like a shark's fin and a front spring housing that resembles a hammerhead's snout. According to Rainey, "It's the first binding that gets plastic boots flexing like they should." And a skier can easily change the binding's pivot point, for easy touring or hardcore backcountry descents.

It's this vacillating nature of backcountry skiing, from lung-busting ascents to heart-pumping turns, that inspired Steve Sullivan and Brian Cousins, founders of Cloudveil Mountain Works, to invent the Serendipity jacket. Named for a long, airy ridge on Mount Owen, in the Tetons, the Serendipity is the closest thing Jackson Hole's skiers have to a

Croakies made by hand, Fuller patented the little neoprene strap and licensed it to Simms' company, Life-Link International.

As for the odd name, it, too, was a ski patrol invention. In the ski resort's early days, the cafeteria made tortilla egg sandwiches. They reminded patroller John Bernadyn of *croques monsieurs*, the French snacks resembling grilled cheese sandwiches. He began to call them croakies. "Grab me a croakie, will ya?" was a common request to any patroller headed to the bottom of the mountain.

Says Simms, "'Croakie' [was] something to eat. Then it got to be anything you couldn't remember the name for." For patrolman Fuller, the name was a perfect fit for his odd little invention.

Croakies are currently sold in more than 30,000 locations, and until the patent ran out a few years ago, Robbie Fuller received a percentage of every neoprene band sold. The invention itself may have little to do with backcountry skiing, but at least it's allowed one Jackson local more time to play in the Tetons.

Left: Steve Markason explores the horizontal backcountry at the Jackson Hole Nordic Center, which comprises fifteen kilometers of groomed trails. Below: Tommy Moe, the first American alpine skier to win two medals in one Winter Olympics, puts the hammer down in Cody Bowl.

mountaineering. He is the guru, the Tetons are his temple, and the back-country around the resort his daily deliverance.

"I don't think any ski resort backcountry compares," he says. "Even in Canada, I doubt any place compares. You have all these big peaks—Cody, No Name, Rendezvous Peak—with extreme skiing off of them, very steep skiing. And you have the big vertical drops like Four Pines, where you can ski a sustained face for well over two thousand vertical feet, not to mention the canyon descents. There are five canyons to the south of the ski area—you can ski in the canyon bottoms and get lots and lots of turns. Or you can milk the canyons' flanks. There's also a beautiful touring route. Staying on a high bench under the peaks, I can guide an intermediate skier all the way to Jensen

Canyon. It's easy terrain, but it's spectacular."

This litany of backcountry delights, moreover, includes only the nine square miles Turiano can legally cover as a guide. To the west, marching toward the hazy fields of Idaho, are more peaks, ridges, and canyons, some hiding oddities such as the Arch Couloir. A two-hour slog from the ski resort, the Arch is just as it sounds—a snowy gully crowned by a rainbow of rock. Immediately to the north of the ski area is Granite Canyon, the

Mike Quinn makes his move.
Once is Enough, 1984.

southernmost drainage of Grand Teton National Park, its ski terrain as glorious as it is treacherous. Striping its southern wall—the northern buttress of the ski resort— is steep chute after steep chute, the names bestowed (ABC Chutes, Endless Couloir, Mile Long Couloir, Air Force Couloir, Spock Chutes, Northwest Passage) laden with meaning for Jackson Hole's boldest skiers.

The drawbacks to skiing Granite Canyon are the interminable traverse back to the ski area ("Lots of times, you forget how good the skiing was by the time you get out," says Turiano) and the avalanche danger. While the couloirs' steepness and northern exposure make for the ultimate in steep, deep powder turns, they also make for insidious

slide conditions. For example, sections of the canyon's north side, opposite Endless and Mile Long couloirs, are occasionally scoured by massive avalanches that rip down the chutes, across the canyon bottom, and up the other side.

Nobody died in a Granite Canyon avalanche until 2000-01, when the new enthusiasm for backcountry skiing and an unstable snowpack met head-on. It was the worst winter on record for avalanche fatalities in Jackson Hole. The snow came fitfully, and as happens in thin

snowpacks, the bottom layers were eaten away by the warmth of the earth, turning rotten and sugary. Without structural strength from below, pockets of consolidated, windblown snow could—and did—slide. There were two avalanche fatalities on Teton Pass, another on the west side of the range, and two in the backcountry close to the ski resort. It was only inevitable that one of those would occur in steep, easily accessible Granite Canyon.

On February 23 at 4 P.M., ski instructor Alan Wagner and three friends headed up the Après Vous quad for a last run. Hiking along the ridge above the chairlift, they traversed into Granite Canyon to ski a steep, two-hundred-foot chute near Caledonia Couloir. Two of the skiers dropped into the chute's right branch and skied to the bottom. Wagner headed left, however, and made only one turn before a thick slab, eighty feet in diameter, cut loose around him. The avalanche swept him over a forty-foot cliff, triggering the snow below to fracture; the whole mass then thundered five hundred feet to the canyon floor below.

Wagner's frantic partners converged on the debris, picked up the signal from his transceiver, located him, and dug three feet down to clear snow from his face—all within five minutes of the avalanche. For the next

James Malkmus takes the express route into Granite Canyon.

forty-five minutes they tried to resuscitate him, but to no avail. Though his partners had done everything right in the aftermath of the slide, Wagner's lifeless body would be flown out of the canyon the next day.

That death—and the death of Ralph Toscano Jr., who was killed in similar circumstances in Rock Springs Canyon, a few hundred yards past a backcountry access gate—sent tremors through the resort and its community of skiers. The message was clear: Do not take the backcountry lightly, especially when the avalanche danger is rated high or considerable, as it had been all winter. Know that even the best preparation and education mean nothing if you ignore obvious warning signs or choose your routes carelessly.

Other incidents during the winter of 2001 showed that avalanches are hardly the backcountry's only dangers. In February, three skiers from Maine spent a frigid night and most of the next day lost in upper Granite Canyon, after becoming disoriented in foggy, snowy conditions. A few weeks later, resort employee Steve Thompson went for a solo afternoon tour in the backcountry—a foolish idea to begin with—and dropped into Granite Canyon thinking it was actually Rock Springs Canyon. Once he realized

Doug Coombs

ENVOY OF THE OUTER LIMITS

Among Jackson skiers, January 22, 1997, is a day that will live in infamy, for that was the day Doug Coombs was kicked off Rendezvous Mountain.

Coombs, once called the "envoy of the outer limits" by *Powder* magazine, is the most famous skier to have cut his teeth in Corbet's Couloir and on Cody Peak. Winner of two World Extreme Skiing Championships, founder of the resort's "steep camps," star of several Teton Gravity Research films, and former owner of Alaska's most popular heli-ski operation, Coombs was the king-pin of the extreme skiing movement, the larger-than-life figure who captured the public's imagination. And a crucial part of that image was his reputation as a rule breaker. But on that wintry day in 1997, the Jackson Hole Ski Patrol decided he'd broken enough rules.

When Coombs arrived in Jackson Hole in 1986, he was a callow Vermont transplant who had learned the tricks of backcountry skiing at Montana's Bridger Bowl, conveniently close to Montana State University. There he'd received a geology degree, and then worked as a geologist for Exxon. But this career didn't last long; while working with a crew of Exxon seismologists in Big Piney, Wyoming, Coombs made repeated weekend forays to Jackson Hole, until he finally realized that oil was a lot less interesting than snow.

His first job after moving to Jackson was as a ski host. "I loved it," he recalls. "It was really a great job. But they didn't invite me back. The clincher was when I skied Central Chute [the couloir bisecting Cody Peak] in my uniform." At his next job, with Teton Video, he and his fellow videographers, stationed on Après Vous, would take turns surreptitiously dropping into nearby Granite Canyon for quick, deep powder runs.

At first, explains Coombs, there were only a handful of locals sneaking into the backcountry, sometimes even in the company of patrollers. "Then people started getting dumb," he says. "They started leaving blatant tracks that tourists could follow. That's when it fell apart." Patrollers began cracking down on backcountry poachers, initiating a cat-and-mouse game that would last for the next decade.

In the meantime, Coombs the ski bum became Coombs the celebrity. Winning the World

Coombs's pass. Coombs argued that he hadn't crossed any closed signs nor skied in any off-limits gully. He suggested that MacKay take a run with him to look at the tracks in question. MacKay refused, and when all was said and done, Coombs had been banished from the ski area for a year-and-a-half.

Coombs still maintains that he wasn't out of bounds on the run. The fact that the patrol moved a closed sign the following day bolsters his argument, he feels. As he said to the *Jackson Hole Guide* at the time, "By moving the sign down the next day, they admitted their guilt. The sign wasn't in the right place. It was a gray area."

"It was definitely not a gray area," countered patrol director Corky Ward in the *Guide*. "He knew what he was doing. In my opinion, he intentionally skied out of bounds. He knows our sign placements better than we do, and my feeling is that when he senses a weak spot in the situation, he should tell us about it instead of exploiting it."

Though locals loudly supported his cause, Coombs didn't stay to plead his case. He moved to Bozeman, Montana, and spent the spring running Valdez Heli Guides. He then continued on to La Grave, France, a ski area without grooming or avalanche control. There he reestablished his steep camps, where he conducts them today.

Doug Coombs

Extreme Skiing Championships in Valdez, Alaska, in 1991, then again in 1993, vaulted Coombs into skiing's stratosphere. He proposed to the ski corporation that he conduct a steep skiing camp. They balked until Coombs wannabes around the country caught wind of the camp. "Pepi [Stiegler] called me in the summer," Coombs recalls. "He said, 'The phone's ringing off the hook!'" By the camp's second year, there were two hundred participants.

The camps caused even more friction with the patrol. Coombs wanted to take his campers on guided backcountry runs and show them how to dig avalanche pits. Repeatedly he asked for back-country access. The patrol gave it, but only grudgingly, he says.

Everything came to a head during the epic winter of 1996-'97. With heavy snows blanketing previously unskiable terrain, local skiers plunged into a feeding frenzy, seeking out any and all untracked lines. The snows also blurred the resort's boundaries, burying normally bare cliffs and closed signs that had to be repeatedly dug out and reerected. It was one of those closed signs that figured significantly in Coombs's expulsion.

Because deep snow had covered a normally rocky barrier, Coombs was able to ski below a closed sign high in the Cirque and drop into a gully near the Headwall, which was closed at the time. When he got to the bottom, patroller Peter MacKay was waiting for him. MacKay, whom Coombs had already nicknamed "Dr. No" for his uncompromising attitude toward the out of bounds, demanded

"It actually worked out really well," says Coombs, who found in La Grave the unregulated skiing he'd wished he'd had in Jackson Hole. Coombs, however, harbors no ill will toward Jackson or its patrol. "All the sourpusses are gone now," he says. And the patrollers seem to have forgotten their grievances with him. In the locker room is a poster advertising Coombs's steep camp in La Grave, with this inscription: "Dear Corky, Thanks for sending me to France!"

Coombs also takes some satisfaction that his expulsion, the ensuing uproar, and patrollers' growing distaste for chasing down poachers helped pave the way for the opening of the backcountry in 1999. His incident was a "catalyst," he says, though he also claims the change was inevitable. "I knew it had to happen," says Coombs. "I just wish I'd been there. That's the one part I'm bummed about—I wasn't there when it opened. But I'm glad it happened, because everybody now enjoys the backcountry for what it is."

he was lost, he struggled back uphill as dusk fell. Afraid to go any farther, Thompson then burrowed into the snow and spent the night fending off hypothermia. The ski patrol found him shakily skiing down the next morning.

"He dodged a bullet, a bigtime bullet," notes ski patrol director Corky Ward. Because the Jackson Hole patrol is best situated to respond to avalanches or accidents in the backcountry nearest the resort, they've agreed to aid Teton County Search and Rescue and national

park rangers in emergencies. But Ward is under no obligation to send patrollers after hurt or lost backcountry skiers if the weather or avalanche conditions preclude safe travel. And he's quick to point out that if things get out of hand, the Forest Service is under no obligation to keep the resort's boundaries open.

"Our entire boundary policy as it exists today could be shut down tomorrow by the national forest," Ward said soon after Thompson's incident. "We're very much in a test period. The public has to treat the policy with respect. It's in their hands to keep the boundaries open."

Treating the policy with respect simply means taking all the most obvious precautions. Ward, his patrollers, and experienced Jackson Hole

Mark Kozac toes the shadow line at Teton Pass.

skiers have little more than contempt for people who pass through backcountry gates without backpacks, which means they're not carrying shovels, the most basic piece of safety gear. Such ignorance means those people are not only a hazard to themselves, but also to anybody who might have to rescue them or who might be below them if they set off a slide.

There is, however, a way to enjoy Jackson Hole's bountiful backcountry even for those whose knowledge of off-piste skiing comes only from the pages of *Skiing* or *Powder*. Emulating the great resorts of Europe, Jackson Hole founders Paul McCollister and Alex Morley long ago established the Alpine Guides, who traditionally led advanced skiers to secret powder stashes inbounds. When the boundary policy changed in 1999, the guides' role expanded to include bringing skiers to the newly accessible backcountry. Culled from Jackson's renowned community of professional mountaineers and fully versed in avalanche science, rescue skills, and first aid, the Alpine Ski and Snowboard Guides have quickly gained favor among visitors who lack backcountry skills but crave a taste of wilderness snow.

Mark Newcomb rides the
slough on No Name Peak.

"It was amazing how many people wanted to utilize our services," says guide Laurie Davis Shepard of the groundbreaking 1999–2000 season. "In 75 percent of our bookings, the clients wanted to go out of bounds."

The guides are only too happy to take them. Mornings start with an early tram ride. Once atop Rendezvous Mountain, guides hand out backpacks, shovels, and avalanche transceivers, then brief their clients on safe backcountry travel practices. Though the guides stay well versed on backcountry snow conditions, there are never any safety guarantees. In fact, some, like senior guide Dave Miller, even explain to clients how to try to outrun a slide.

"What I like to do is point it downhill to pick up speed, then zip out," Dave said to two Australian guests one morning. "You probably have three seconds. The problem is when people go Gumby and start yelling 'Oh, avalanche, avalanche,' and then they're in it."

After some practice with transceivers, the parties strike out for the wild beyond. For many parties, such as the Ferrer family from Greenwich, Connecticut, who joined Tom Turiano for a week of touring in March

Above: The west side of Cody Peak offers far different skiing than the craggy eastern and southern sides. Right: Jason Tattersall cloaks himself in "Wyoming smoke."

2001, it was the first backcountry snow they'd experienced.

"It's a great option," said Carlos Ferrer, an investment banker. "I don't know if I'd do it on a regular basis, especially if the snow was really good on the resort's frontside, but I had to bring my family out to try it."

Of course, it helped that his wife, Rosemary, daughter, Annie, and son, Willie, could all ski well. And it helped that Turiano could gauge how far out he could take the

Ferrers and what kind of terrain they could handle. But Turiano didn't baby them. The Ferrers' excursion to Four Pines included two arduous ascents with their skis on their backs, as they followed Turiano on steep trails stomped into the snow by previous ski parties. Earning your turns is the rule in the backcountry, but for the Ferrers, it was a new experience with its own rewards.

"What I'm starting to appreciate," said Carlos as he followed Annie to the top of Four Pines, "is that hiking becomes as much fun as skiing. But you don't pick that up overnight. It kind of grows on you."

Carlos had a daunting experience on his first backcountry hike at Jackson Hole. During a ski trip earlier that winter, he and

several friends hired Turiano, Kent McBride, and a few other guides to lead them up Cody Peak for a powder run down No Shadows. The prospect of skiing from the top of Jackson Hole's signature back-country peak was enticing; the process of getting up there, on a precarious, rocky route that skirted some significant vertical drops, was less fun than it looked.

"I didn't recognize it at the time," said Carlos, "but I had a little vertigo issue. You know what I did? I hugged the earth. I didn't move. I said to Kent, 'I think I better go back.' He said, 'No way. Get yourself up. Get erect so you can dig your toes into the snow. Keep your head down. Don't look to either side. And keep stepping.'"

"McBride was right," continued Carlos of his first experience climbing in ski boots. "You've got to keep moving. You have to stand tall."

Thanks to the resort's open-boundary policy, the temptation to go O.B. is always there, symbolized by stark and magnificent Cody Peak. But skiers must think hard before succumbing to the siren call of somebody else's tracks looping down Four Shadows or Cody Bowl. We all live to make such turns, but they're never worth dying for. ❄

Left: Eric Otterholt drops into Pucker Face, the east-facing flank of Cody's north ridge. Above: Jeremy Jones looks for his landing on a line in Rock Springs Canyon that locals affectionately call "Fat Bastard."

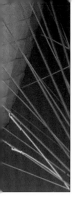

chapter 8

SUMMER IN
JACKSON HOLE

The stream begins a few miles northwest of Jackson Hole Mountain Resort, in a high, lonely basin just below the crest of the Teton Range. It has no definite origin; here and there rivulets trickle out from under melting snowfields, which in May and June have been hardened on top by the spring sun and hollowed out underneath by the warmth of the earth. As the stream follows its cobbled bed, it gains volume and breadth from other rivulets, from other snow still plastered against the flanks of mountains or heaped on their summits.

Walls rise on either side of the stream—black buttresses, gleaming wet. It is from these dark walls that the chasm, known as Death Canyon, probably got its name, though some historians hold that the name came after a member of an early expedition— either the Hayden Survey of 1872 or the Bannon Survey of 1903—wandered into the canyon, never to be seen again.

Where the walls draw together closest, darkening the stream with their shadows, the canyon suddenly loses its floor and drops toward Jackson Hole. At that point the stream erupts, leaping from rock to rock, frothing and roaring. In June, there is no better show in the Tetons. By comparison, Hidden Falls in Cascade Canyon is just a wall of water, a drama in two dimensions. Death Canyon Creek, on the other hand, is a spitting, writhing serpent, its angry roar amplified by the thousand-foot walls towering over it.

In this torrent one might find a metaphor for summer in Jackson Hole. The valley, after all, is one of the most heavily visited vacation spots in North America. At least four million people pass through each year, and most of them come during July and August. The town bustles; Yellowstone and Grand Teton National Parks revive from their winter doldrums; the highways hum. And yet there are more means of escape in summer than in winter. Besides trails, rivers, and back roads, there's an artistic culture that revels in the warm weather. One can get lost in art, music, or drama; lost in the crowds in Jackson's town square; or simply lost. Summer in Jackson Hole knows no bounds other thani its own brevity. Its mirror image is the stream through Death Canyon. It's chaotic yet calming, perennial yet ephemeral. And it rushes past faster than the eye can follow.

Melting snow, of course, begets more than sound and fury. As the remaining patches of snow crawl higher up the mountainsides, wildflowers follow, blooming first

Scott Harris, under the yellow wing, and Tom Bartlett, under the pink one, soar over Rendezvous Mountain in search of "house thermals," columns of rising air consistently found over specific ridges or slopes.

Left: For most of the summer, the Aerial Tram operates from 9 A.M. to 7 P.M.
Below: More than twenty companies in and around Jackson offer
guided float trips on the mighty Snake River.

on the valley floor, then appearing at steadily higher elevations as the weather warms. Winter's whites and grays may be elegant, but nobody can deny the luminosity of the Tetons' wildflowers, not even the skiers who despair at seeing the snows go.

Truly desperate skiers continue to ride the resort's aerial tram well into the summer, as long as patches of snow remain on the high peaks of the backcountry. Clomping onto the tram in ski boots, they certainly surprise the tourists making the 4,139-vertical-foot journey for the views, the hikes, and the flowers. There's no better way, actually, to appreciate the full range of the wildflower season, as the tram carries passengers straight from the mountain shrub vegetative community to the Alpine zone. Gaining the

same elevation on foot would leave most visitors sorely indisposed to appreciate the blooms around them.

Wildflowers, however, are only part of Jackson Hole's vegetative story. A recorded message that plays during the aerial tram's summer journeys claims that 125 species of plants dwell within the resort's boundaries. But between 1996 and 2000, botanist and photographer Charmaine Delmatier did an exhaustive survey of the plants on Rendezvous

The Kemmerers
STEWARDS FOR A NEW ERA

When the Kemmerer family—John "Jay" Kemmerer III and his sisters, Connie Kemmerer and Betty Kemmerer Gray—bought Jackson Hole Ski Resort in 1992, their new acquisition was woefully behind the times. Snowmaking was scant, lifts were slow, and intermediate terrain was not easily accessible. Locals and expert skiers loved the mountain; nearly everybody else ignored it.

What could not be ignored, however, was its potential. The Tetons, embracing one national park and abutting another, are America's mountains. The appeal of a ski resort in such a range goes deeper than steepness or size; it beckons to basic sentiments of independence, ruggedness, and fearlessness.

The Kemmerers recognized this; they also had their own sentiments to answer to. Having extracted nearly a century's worth of coal from their mines in southwestern Wyoming, and having sold the Kemmerer Coal Company in 1981, they were anxious to reestablish ties with Wyoming and to find an investment that could be as economically advantageous to the state as the state had been to them. Moreover, as full-time Teton Village resident Connie Kemmerer explains, "We're a family, and we thought we'd be appropriate owners following the McCollisters. We liked the idea of it staying a family business."

But while Paul McCollister struggled throughout his ownership to keep the resort afloat and to make crucial upgrades, the Kemmerers have been able to afford a host of improvements. In 1994 they replaced the aging Thunder double chair with a quad; in 1996 they installed the Teewinot high-speed quad; in 1997 they built the Bridger gondola and Bridger Center, and in 1999 they installed extensive snowmaking and the Après Vous high-speed quad.

"The mountain was not balanced properly," explains Jay Kemmerer,

yurts in the resort's backcountry. More importantly, now that Rendezvous Mountain's lifts have been brought up to speed, Teton Village must catch up, a much more complex process. The village, says Kemmerer, cannot simply attract visitors to the ski mountain; it has to attract visitors to itself. "It needs an amenity base of several several different dining experiences, barber shops, drug stores, churches, a meeting center," he notes. "It needs things to make it a community."

What the Kemmerers fear most is Teton Village turning into a ghost resort of high-end homes and condominiums whose owners refuse to rent when they're absent. First steps have been taken to circumvent that possibility, namely the construction of the fractional-ownership Teton Club, and the resort's investment in the new Four Seasons Resort Jackson Hole. Jackson locals may not consider these the most inclusive establishments, but they do create "hot beds," a favorite term of Kemmerer's, meaning beds not left empty for all but two weeks of the year.

"The Four Seasons is a very important project," says Kemmerer. "It creates hot beds, it creates a quality level this area hasn't seen. We like that. But we're not just trying to advocate the high end here, we're not trying to be a Deer Valley. The Hostel X is almost as important. You've got to have the Hostel too." Agrees Connie Kemmerer, "We want this to be a resort for everybody, not just the rich and famous."

The Kemmerers hope that, with several different hands shaping its future, the village will attain its own eclectic character in the manner of Jackson's town square. But they'd also like to insure that the future village "has the right light angles, not dark corridors and big buildings with cold surfaces," Jay Kemmerer says. "It needs

Jay and Connie Kemmerer

who lives most of the year in New Jersey. "When we built the gondola, that changed the whole dynamics of the skier patterns. Without restaurants on the mountain, we needed a way for people to easily get back up the mountain. The gondola also addressed our reputation as being cold—it's warm, and it's more social."

The owners have spent nearly $55 million on these improvements and others, a huge sum given Jackson Hole's skier numbers. "The Kemmerer family needed to investment-spend to create the momentum for a success here," says Jay Kemmerer. "Right now we have more skier capacity than our visits warrant. We need to let the visits start catching up." The problem, he says, is that skier demographics are changing. "Skiers are getting older, they're more often female, and the number of days they spend skiing per trip is decreasing . . . and now, with Jackson's second-home market, people are coming in and not skiing at all."

To counter this, the Kemmerers hope to introduce more ways to allow people to enjoy Rendezvous Mountain, such as establishing a system of

to be well thought out and designed and planned. For a company that's not overly profitable to try and have that vision, it takes time."

The Kemmerers insist they have time, that they can wait for their investment to pay off. "Our family was involved for a long time in the coal-mining business," says Jay Kemmerer. "We're not a flip kind of family. I've made investments, then sold them. I've done leveraged buyouts. I don't have those intentions here. We are proud of our Wyoming heritage and want Wyoming to be proud of us."

Which means that the community's most persistent rumor—that Vail is going to buy Jackson Hole Mountain Resort—can be quelled. Jay Kemmerer reports that he has received "multiple inquiries" from the owners of Vail, "but the answer's always the same."

So, too, can another rumor be quashed: that Teton Village's treasured clock tower is going to be torn down. Though Paul McCollister's Alpine steeple is out of style with the Village's current western theme, Jay Kemmerer considers the clock tower a strong symbol of the resort, and its destruction "is not part of any plans I know of."

"You keep your roots," he says. "You don't tear them up and throw them away."

Right: Moose calves are usually born in early summer, so that's when their mothers are most protective—and—dangerous. Below: Mountain biking on the west side of the range, near Grand Targhee Ski Resort. Far right: Maria Oksanen enjoys the stillness of early morning on Jackson Lake.

Mountain. She discovered that there were almost four times as many species—468, to be exact—as previously thought.

The growing season is brief, but the sun, soil, seeds, and snowmelt waste no time. The result is a panoply of trees, shrubs, sedges, and flowers, their names as distinctive, even riotous, as their blooms. At the ski resort's lowest reaches grow such plants as mountain snowberry, cow parsnip, Colorado columbine, western larkspur, western coneflower, huckleberry, bitterbrush, chokecherry, twinberry, elderberry, and Saskatoon serviceberry.

Higher on the mountain are nine types of orchids (including the rare broadleafed twayblade), spleenwort (also rare), elephant heads, explorer gentian, and the elegant death camas, a cream-colored flower as

beautiful as it is poisonous. Providing shade for the berries and Oregon grape beneath them are Engelmann spruce, blue spruce, Douglas fir, and limber pine. Still higher, gnarled and hardy whitebark pine are the predominant conifers.

Generally, plants are more diminutive the higher the elevation. In the Alpine zone, according to Delmatier, many plants barely reach two inches in height, the better to survive the whipping winds, cold temperatures, and extremely short growing season (mid-July to

mid-August). "Many of the plants are rosettes," she says, "because they have to flower, set seed, and produce fruit, all within a very narrow window of time."

However small, these plants more than stand up for themselves in beauty. Among Delmatier's favorites are moss campion, which creates wide carpets of pink, and *Saxifraga oppositifolia*. "That's one of the most unique plants I've ever seen," she says, "because it's the only rectangular plant up there—it's not round

at all. Also, it's locally rare—it's found elsewhere in the Tetons and other ranges but at the ski resort, it's found only in Cody Bowl [the broad basin under Cody's triangular summit]. Actually, when you get into Cody Bowl, you find all these spectacular little alpine flowers you don't see on the rest of the mountain."

These weird little flowers—let's not forget the rare rock cress draba and the aromatic pussytoes—come late in the summer, long after Jackson Hole has traditionally kicked off the season. Notwithstanding the sometimes wintry weather, summer officially begins on Memorial Day weekend, when the town of Jackson celebrates Old West Days, and a circle of tepees and canvas tents springs up in a meadow near Teton Village.

This isn't a shantytown for seasonal waitresses and retail clerks,

Right: A bird's eye view of a paraglider above Rendezvous Mountain. Below: A cyclist in full racing trim during the Pole Pedal Paddle, Jackson Hole's signature multi-sport race, held every April. Far right: Franz Kessler high on the east ridge of the Grand Teton.

although the deepening dearth of affordable housing in the valley may eventually call for one. Rather, the anachronistic camp is the setting for the Mountain Man Rendezvous, which recalls the gatherings of the mountain men in the first half of the nineteenth century. Actually, trappers never rendezvoused below Rendezvous Peak or Rendezvous Mountain. But they did gather in June of 1832 in Pierre's Hole, just on the other side of the Tetons (Pierre's Hole is now Teton Valley, Idaho). There they sold pelts, traded news, gambled, and drank.

"The early mountain man rendezvous were just drunken orgies," says Lee Williamson, a tall, grandfatherly "mountain man" from Ogden, Utah, who is a veteran of gatherings such as Jackson's rendezvous. "They

hadn't had whiskey all winter, so all they did was drink and fight. But that's not the way it works today. We come back again and again, we bring our families, we protect each other."

The event at Teton Village is one of several dozen reenactments that occur each year in the West. Indeed, an entire subculture exists of modern mountain men and women who feel that they're closer in spirit to Lewis and Clark than to most twenty-first-century Americans. Armed with homemade hunting

and camping equipment—tepees, bedrolls, muskets, bows—and clad in beads and moccasins, they travel throughout the spring and summer from rendezvous to rendezvous. The "tour" begins on Easter weekend at Ogden, Utah, and ends on Labor Day, when hundreds of reenactment aficionados gather near Evanston, Wyoming, their games, contests, storytelling sessions, and trading booths attracting tens of thousands of curious "flatlanders," as they call the rest of us.

Though the gathering at Teton Village is more modest, it still looks and smells genuine, the scent of pine smoke and freshly tanned leather permeating the canvas tents, where participants sell beads, trinkets, carvings, pelts, and fringed deer-hide jackets. These are the gleanings from their winters, which some indeed spend in primitive dwellings, way out in the woods.

"That's Rabbit," says Williamson, pointing out a thin, bearded fellow wrapped in a wool blanket. "He's a genuine mountain man. He's true blue. I think he finally built a cabin, but he lived in a tepee for ten years before that."

Most of the mountain men, however, lead double lives, holding

Above: Participants in the Mountain Man Rendezvous try to be as "period" as possible, keeping their clothing and camping gear consistent with what was used in the 1840s. Right: J.R. Stotts, a.k.a "Teaspoon," unleashes an arrow.

down normal occupations when not rendezvousing. One such is J.R. Stotts, an auto mechanic from Roy, Utah. Here among his mountain man peers, he's "Teaspoon," a skilled archer and beadworker who gained his name six years ago, at his first rendezvous, when he was seen loading gunpowder into a musket with a plastic teaspoon.

"This life can grow on a person real quick," says Teaspoon, showing a guest the interior of his immaculately kept tepee. "People at work tell me I was born 150 years too late. And I was. If I could live like this twelve months a year, if I didn't have that three-letter-word, j-o-b, I'd be in here."

Or he'd be outside, practicing his tomahawk throwing and archery for the contests that are part of every rendezvous. Such competi-

tions are just as important to the participants as selling handicrafts. Unfortunately, not all of the contests are allowed at the Teton Village rendezvous, which rankles a mountain man called "Digger." In his opinion, the Jackson Hole gathering is a "dog and pony show" because it lacks a black powder riflery contest. "It's the condominiums," he says. "The owners don't want holes shot in the sides of their condos. Pretty narrow-minded, I'd say."

Musket fire may not be music to most

Teton Village has hosted the
Mountain Man Rendezvous
for more than a decade.
Left: Yellow Mule's Ears
grow next to a charred log in
Grand Teton National Park.
Right: Stephanie Tanner,
Teaspoon's stepdaughter.

people's ears; for those with more refined aural tastes, Teton Village has long provided a sophisticated summer salve. Once the mountain men leave, the classical musicians come, bringing their own handcrafted contrivances—violins, cellos, oboes, and kettle drums—for a series of concerts running from the Fourth of July weekend through the end of August.

In 1962 a local fine-arts guild established a Jackson Hole Fine Arts Festival, which featured dance, film, visual art, and classical music. The ear-

liest orchestral performances were held in the Jackson Hole High School gymnasium; in subsequent summers, the festival's orchestra also played at Jackson Lake Lodge, on the lawn of St. John's Episcopal Church, in Jackson's town square, and, in 1967, in a tent at Teton Village. There was even the occasional chamber performance at the Mangy Moose Saloon.

Eventually the summer gathering of musicians was dubbed the Grand Teton Musical Festival and was given a permanent home in the center of Teton Village. In 1974, with land donated by Paul McCollister, architect Bob Corbett (one of those responsible for the village's original layout) and acoustician Christopher Jaffe created the Walk Festival Hall. Named for Margaretha Walk, festival business manager and wife of

longtime conductor Ling Tung, the hall, according to the festival's present director, Don Reinhold, is "an acoustic phenomenon." He adds, "You might think the hall doesn't look like anything special, but it's like a musical instrument itself. The acoustics inside are just incredible. Some of our musicians, who've played in every famous hall in the world, say Walk is their favorite place to play."

Acoustics, of course, mean little without musicians to employ them. Over the years, Tung (who retired in 1996), present music director Eiji Oue, and the festival's staff have gathered a virtuoso orchestra of musicians from around the country, so highly regarded that in 2001, National Public Radio broadcast the season's first series of concerts live

on "Performance Today." It may have been the ultimate validation of Tung's, Oue's, and Reinhold's ambitions for their summer festival to be regarded as one of the nation's finest.

Then again, the Grand Teton Music Festival need look no farther than its own community for validation. It's no mean feat to lure Jackson locals inside, for any reason, on a warm summer's evening. This is a year-round, morning-to-night outdoor community of not only audacious skiers but also some of the finest mountaineers,

Far left: Jackson Hole Trail Rides offers horseback excursions from Teton Village to Granite Canyon and Phelps Lake, in Grand Teton National Park. Left and above: Jackson Hole Mountain Resort has begun to build mountain bike trails on Rendezvous Mountain and will eventually have 20 miles of lift-accessed trails.

whitewater kayakers, mountain bikers, triathletes, paragliders, fly-fishermen, landscape painters, and wildlife photographers in the country, all of whom find inspiration—athletic and aesthetic—in Wyoming's wide open spaces.

All the locals are like walking advertisements, hoping to coax old friends visiting from out of town, new residents, or total strangers into sampling their favorite flavor of adrenaline. Each summertime pursuit seduces participants with its own mixture of sound, smell, scenery, mental

trials, and muscular ache. Climbing the Grand Teton, for instance, brings with it the sleepiness of a predawn awakening, the feel of warm stone underhand, the breathlessness of altitude, the steeling of one's nerves against a great space yawning below, the clank of carabiners, and the curious anticlimax of reaching the summit and finding no more rock to climb.

There are, of course, definite rewards to reaching the Grand's 13,770-foot summit (second only in height in Wyoming to 13,804-foot Gannett Peak, in the Wind River Range). There's the sense of accomplishment, for one. There's the rare, eye-level view of Gannett, seventy miles away. And there's the even more arresting

Above: Hikers in summer can follow the seven-mile-long road to the summit of Rendezvous Mountain, then ride the tram back down for free. Left: The Snake, home to the indigenous Fine-spotted Snake River Cutthroat, is one of the West's last truly wild fisheries.

view, almost directly below, of the Snake River's serpentine gleam.

Starting in Yellowstone Park, filling Jackson Lake, then draining south to begin a thousand-mile journey to its confluence with the Columbia River, the Snake is Jackson Hole's second great physical feature next to the Grand Teton. Those intent on finding whitewater or trout would call it the first. It is, in fact, many things to many beings, human and otherwise. The Snake is a natural roller-coaster for paddlers, a life-giving artery to farmers and ranchers, a home to cutthroat and brown trout, a foraging ground for moose, and a hunting ground for ospreys and bald eagles. It also provides one of the easiest ways, in addition to hiking or climbing, for us to escape

our mechanized world. As naturalist Loren Eiseley wrote, "If there is magic on this planet, it is contained in water."

River guide Matt Hansen has seen the water work its magic countless times. It's worked on him: Hansen was a rafting guide for three years, gave it up to be a reporter at the *Jackson Hole Guide*, then quit to go back to guiding. Though rowing the intricately braided stretch of the Snake through Grand Teton National Park is wearying, Hansen is renewed daily by the river's

Right: Mountain biking in September, which can bring either hot sun or wind and snow. Below: Originally called the Mangy Moose Spaghetti Emporium, Saloon, and Opera House, the Moose was founded in 1967 and enlarged in 1987.

effect on his passengers, the majority of whom have never been on a wild river before.

"Sometimes, older people on the boat see a bald eagle and tell me that's the first bald eagle they've ever seen in their lives," says Hansen. "Or they see moose, and they're speechless. That's the thing about the river I love the most. It's so quiet, like a church or a library. Nobody raises their voice. It's as if the river and everything around it command automatic respect."

Water, however, is not the only liquid

medium navigable by humans. There's the sky itself, a playground for paragliders. Though in its infancy compared to river-running, mountaineering, or fly-fishing, paragliding reaches back to the most ancient of human aspirations: to simply trot off a hilltop and fly.

"It's definitely not just an adrenaline sport," says Tom Bartlett, who co-manages the tandem paragliding operation at Jackson Hole Mountain Resort. "It means a lot more to me than that. It's flying, you know? Like a bird."

Bartlett, who ski patrols at the resort in the winter, has been flying for fourteen years. He knows intimately the weather and wind patterns above the Tetons. Like every experienced paraglider, he's as

much a meteorologist as a pilot, and any discussion he enters into about the flying conditions at Teton Village soon becomes a tangle of terms like "venturi winds," "convergence," and "thermal turbulence." All his passengers need to know is that he's never had an accident, nor deployed his reserve chute. He'll strap anyone to the front of his harness, he says, who weighs between 75 and 240 pounds and is athletic enough to sprint ten or twenty yards at the takeoff.

The takeoffs occur, of course, at the summit of Rendezvous Mountain, taking full advantage of the aerial tram's vertical rise, "the highest of any tandem operation in the country," according to Bartlett. Early in the morning, before the sun has warmed the earth, he and his

passengers float the 4,139 vertical feet to the base of the mountain. Bartlett calls these early flights "sled rides," since the paraglider drifts gradually downward on the cool air to a landing zone by Teton Village. But as the day progresses, the earth's warmth and the mountains' topography create updrafts. The result is more turbulence ("We don't recommend these flights to people who get airsick easily," says Bartlett) but also more lift. When piloting his tandem wing, Bartlett can use these thermals to turn a twenty-minute ride into an

hour-long one. Solo paragliders, adept at finding and riding thermals—the trick is to circle within them, spiraling upward until the elevation cools and stalls the rising air—have flown all the way from Teton Village to Pinedale, Wyoming, seventy-two miles away.

For a first-time paraglider, however, the distance covered means less than a new perspective discovered. Or rediscovered. Paragliding is eerily similar to the flights in one's dreams. There's no sound but the wind. Beyond one's

free-hanging feet the landscape is strangely askew. And the birds—fellow aeronauts—show no fear.

"I've had bald eagles flying five yards away from me in the same thermal," says Bartlett. "It's pretty cool. The hawks and eagles don't seem to mind us there."

Perhaps they know that for humans, the act of flight requires all of our attention. Or perhaps their trust is related to the season. Thermals, after all, are a warm-weather phenomenon, and summer in the Tetons is all too brief. It's not hard to believe that the raptors, like humans, enjoy some company when reaping the season's fleeting rewards. 🌺

Last TRAM

Above and left: Stick out your tongue and say, "Yee ha!" Right: The season is over, marked by a volley of snowballs.

This is where it all ends: a tramcar filled with fifty-four hell-bent, wild-eyed skiers and snowboarders, everybody's face seamed by a loopy grin. It's 3:30 P.M., April 8, the last day of the 2000-01 season, and "last tram" is about to leave the dock in Teton Village. The automatic doors close, the tram eases from the dock, and everybody in unison lets loose a howl. Snowballs, thrown by those who couldn't get on last tram, thwack against the car's walls and windows—their report raises an even louder howl. From the ground, we on last tram must sound like madmen, inmates confined to a crowded red asylum tethered to the sky. Somebody shouts, "Spark it up!" Several passengers, sedatives already in hand, comply, and we head for Rendezvous's summit wreathed by redolent smoke.

A spot on last tram is the most coveted of the winter season, even more so than a spot on the first tram of the winter, when Rendezvous Bowl's powder is untouched. To be among the tram's final customers—you have to get in line at just the right time, not so early that you are herded onto the 3:18 tram, not so late that you are left at the bottom until next December—is a final testament to one's commitment to this ski mountain and to winter itself. It shows you've stayed to the bitter end, have wrested every last vertical foot of powder, hardpack, and corn that Rendezvous Mountain might offer, and will not be turned away from the playground until you are dragged kicking and screaming from the premises.

Nobody, however, is leaving unsatisfied today, even those left in the tram maze, looking slightly dazed, when the ticket checker clamps shut the tram dock's steel gate for the last time. It's been the closing day of a lifetime. This morning we woke to eight inches of fresh, light snow atop Rendezvous Mountain, on the heels of twelve inches of snow just four days before. Though it's the last month of a fairly dry winter—snow depths are only 60 percent of what they usually are this time of year—the mountain has been renewed. The storm was a final, conciliatory gift from Ullr, the Norse snow god, and his Jackson acolytes have been partaking of it with religious zeal.

I haven't skied so hard all season. Finally, at the end of winter, my legs and turns are honed. I feel bulletproof today, able to fire off telemark turns from top to bottom and to keep up with the snowboarders and alpine skiers who are similarly steeled and stoked. A half dozen of us have skied in an adrenalized rat pack, revisiting all the favorites—the Far Drift on Rendezvous Bowl, Cheyenne Woods, Toilet Bowl, Bernie's Bowl—and hitting a few lines only lately filled in with adequate snow—Alta Chutes, No-No Chute, Expert Chutes.

Everybody on the mountain is ebullient. Says Matt

Wilkens, a fellow passenger on last tram, "Good things come to those who wait."

Sometimes the wait this winter felt long. January's snowfall was scant. Today is the January we never had. Indeed, everybody is bundled up as if it's midwinter; only a few are in closing-day costumes, including an Elvis Presley, complete with white jumpsuit and cape, riding on custom Elvis Presley skis. The least bundled, as usual, are Marvin Howard and the other members of the Teton Nude Descent Club, who always make a goosepimpled appearance on the season's final day. Not even subfreezing temperatures dissuaded them today from their full frontal attack on Amphitheater Run.

"At least there's a good tailwind," Howard will remark to a photographer before his run.

"Tower three!" somebody shouts out on the tram. We're halfway up the mountain, halfway through the ride. Passengers are stomping on the car's floor. Whiskey flasks make their way around. Music blares. Last night, "Grateful" Dave Wilcox rifled through his tapes, looking for the ideal last tram accompaniment. He found it and gave the tape to the tram operator when he boarded. "Hear this?" he shouts to me over the din. "This is the first time the Dead ever played this live." The choice, indeed, is perfect: "Fire on the Mountain."

The tram sails over the Expert Chutes, where earlier I had the run of the day, maybe even the season. It was the first time all winter I climbed to the two farthest, highest chutes, Claustrophobia and Insomnia. After a few spongy turns down the top of Claustrophobia, above the cliffs, I pointed my skis downhill through the "pinch," then sank into five turns of neck-deep nirvana. In those five turns was all the truth and beauty of powder skiing. Five turns to last a lifetime. Or at least a summer.

The tram crests the final cliffs. Ringing the tram dock is a crowd of fifty people, everybody cradling chunks of snow. This is the winter's final tradition—the bombardment of last tram's passengers as they disembark. As the tram slows before the dock, the yelling inside calms to a few quiet laughs, the bleats of lambs going to slaughter. Then the doors open, and everybody pushes out on to the dock, into a hail of snowballs.

Ullr shows his mercy again. The snow is too cold to make the sort of missiles that have been fired at last trammers in the past. We clomp down the stairs, wielding our skis and snowboards like shields. A snowball grazes my head, then the fusillade is over. The season is over. The sun is dropping toward Idaho, the lifts below are still, and we stand on the mountain and laugh.

Thanks to Bill Grout and his talented team of booksmiths at Mountain Sports Press—Michelle Schrantz, Scott Kronberg, Alan Stark, Cindy Hirschfeld, and Mark Doolittle. Special thanks also to Vicki Arundale for conceiving this book; Connie Kemmerer for helping make it happen; Anna Olson and Shannon Brooks of Jackson Hole Mountain Resort; Jill Russell and the Jackson Hole Historical Society; Pepi Stiegler; Corky Ward, Greg Miles, Cindy Budge, Kirby Williams, Tom Bartlett, and the members of the Jackson Hole Ski Patrol; Rod Newcomb; Teton Gravity Research; Thomas Turiano; Angus M. Thuermer, Jr.; Alex Morley; Mike McCollister; Roger Brown; Barry Corbet; Gene Downer; Mike and Benny Wilson; Steve Barker; Bissell Hazen; Tom Bie; photographers Wade McKoy, Bob Woodall, Carl Oksanen, Jim Elder, Fletcher Manley, Bruce Morley, Greg Von Doersten, Florence McCall, Chris Figenshau, Jonathan Selkowitz, John Layshock, David O'Conner, Jeff Diener, Andrew McGarry, and Bill Scott, who had the prescience to shoot color slides of the Crystal Springs Ranch nearly fifty years ago; Christian Beckwith for the race (though he won); my unfailingly supportive parents and sisters; and my infinitely patient housemates in the little green house —Nicole Stokes, Aaron Foreman, Scott Fabrizio, and Bodhi.

"How can you write a book about a ski area if you don't go skiing?" Credit—or discredit—should also go to Rob Werner, Jimmy Chin, Jeff Stein, Jimmy Hartman, Evan Howe, Chris McCollister, Cory Buenning, Brendan O'Neil, and other ski partners for repeatedly and gleefully distracting me from my task. A bigger season and this book may never have been finished.

Sources:

Along the Ramparts of the Tetons, The Saga of Jackson Hole, Wyoming, by Robert B. Betts, Colorado Associated University Press, 1978.

Teton Skiing, A History and Guide to the Teton Range, by Thomas Turiano, Homestead Publishing, 1995.

Teton Tales and Other Petzoldt Anecdotes, by Paul K. Petzoldt, ICS Books, 1995.

The Pass, Historic Teton Pass and Wilson, Wyoming, by Doris B. Platts, 1988.

This Was Jackson Hole, by Fern K. Nelson, High Plains Press, 1994.

Teton Magazine and *Teton Annual*

Jackson Hole Magazine

Jackson Hole News

Jackson Hole Guide

Jackson's Hole Courier

Cover — Jason Tattersall by Bob Woodall
p. 1 — Kristina Olson by Chris Figenshau
pp. 2, 3 — Rob Haggart by Wade McKoy
p. 7 — David Gonzales
p. 8 — Dan Treadway by Andrew McGarry
p. 11 — Florence McCall

First Box
p. 12 — Bob Woodall
p. 13 (both) — David Gonzales

Chapter One
p. 15 — Carl Oksanen
p. 16 (top) — Carl Oksanen
p. 16 (bottom) — Jackson Hole Historical Society
p. 17 (both) — Jackson Hole Historical Society
pp. 18, 19 — Carl Oksanen
p. 20 — Jim Elder
p. 21 (top) — Jackson Hole Historical Society
p. 21 (middle) — Jackson Hole Historical Society
p. 21 (bottom) — Florence McCall
p. 22 (top) — Carl Oksanen
p. 22 (bottom) — Bob Woodall
p. 23 — Carl Oksanen
p. 24 — Carl Oksanen
p. 25 — Carl Oksanen
p. 26 (both) — Bill Scott
p. 27 — Jackson Hole Historical Society

Chapter Two
p. 29 — Carl Oksanen
p. 30 — Jackson Hole Historical Society
p. 31 (both) — Jackson Hole Historical Society
p. 32 — Jackson Hole Historical Society
p. 33 (both) — Jackson Hole Historical Society
p. 34 — Jackson Hole Historical Society
p. 35 — SKI Magazine archives
p. 36 — Jackson Hole Historical Society
p. 37 (top) — Carl Oksanen
p. 37 (bottom) — Florence McCall
p. 38 — Bob Woodall
p. 39 — Fletcher Manley
p. 40 — Bob Woodall
p. 41 — Bob Woodall

Chapter Three
p. 43 — Jackson Hole Mountain Resort archives
p. 44 (all) — Jim Elder
p. 45 — Jim Elder
p. 46 — Jackson Hole Mountain Resort archives
p. 47 — Jim Elder
p. 48 — Jackson Hole Mountain Resort archives
p. 49 — Skiing Magazine archives
p. 50 (both) — Jackson Hole Mountain Resort archives
p. 51 — Jackson Hole Mountain Resort archives
p. 52 — Jim Elder
p. 53 — Jim Elder
p. 54 — Jackson Hole Mountain Resort archives
p. 55 (top) — Jim Elder
p. 55 (bottom) — Gene Downer collection
p. 56 — Fletcher Manley
p. 57 — Jim Elder

Chapter Four
p. 59 — Bob Woodall
p. 60 (left) — Jim Elder
p. 60 (right) — SKI Magazine archives
p. 61 — Fletcher Manley
p. 62 (both) — Pepi Stiegler collection
p. 63 — Jim Elder
p. 64 (top left) — Jim Elder
p. 64 (top right) — Fletcher Manley
p. 64 (bottom) — Fletcher Manley
p. 65 (top) — Fletcher Manley
p. 65 (bottom left) — Fletcher Manley
p. 65 (bottom right) — Jim Elder

p. 66 — Wade McKoy
p. 67 — Wade McKoy
p. 68 (left) — Wade McKoy
p. 68 (right) — SKIING Magazine archives
p. 69 — Fletcher Manley
p. 70 (left) — Jackson Hole Mountain Resort archives
p. 70 (right) — Pepi Stiegler
p. 71 — Bruce Morley
p. 72 — Jim Elder
p. 73 (top) — Greg Von Doersten
p. 73 (bottom) — Fletcher Manley
p. 74 — Wade McKoy
p. 75 (top left) — Fletcher Manley
p. 75 (top right) — Fletcher Manley
p. 75 (bottom) — Jackson Hole Mountain Resort archives
p. 76 — Bob Woodall
p. 77 (top) — Wade McKoy
p. 77 (bottom) — Jim Elder
p. 78 — Wade McKoy
p. 79 — Bob Woodall
p. 80 — Jim Elder
p. 81 (both) — Bruce Morley
p. 82 — David Gonzales
p. 83 — Bob Woodall
p. 84 — Bruce Morley
p. 85 — Wade McKoy
p. 86 — Wade McKoy
p. 87 — Bob Woodall
p. 88 — Ted Wood
p. 89 — John Layshock

Chapter Five
p. 91 — Bob Woodall
p. 92 (top) — Bob Woodall
p. 92 (bottom) — David Gonzales
p. 93 — Bob Woodall
p. 94 (top) — Wade McKoy
p. 94 (bottom) — Florence McCall
p. 95 (top left) — Wade McKoy
p. 95 (top right) — Florence McCall
p. 95 (bottom) — John Layshock
p. 96 — Fletcher Manley
p. 97 — Fletcher Manley
p. 98 — Fletcher Manley
p. 99 (both) — Fletcher Manley
p. 100 — Fletcher Manley
p. 101 — Florence McCall
p. 102 (left) — Jonathan Selkowitz
p. 102 (right) — Wade McKoy
p. 103 (top) — David Gonzales
p. 103 (bottom) — Florence McCall
p. 104 (top) — Fletcher Manley
p. 104 (bottom) — Florence McCall
p. 105 — Greg Von Doersten
p. 106 (both) — Wade McKoy
p. 107 — David Gonzales
p. 108 — Bob Woodall
p. 109 — Wade McKoy
p. 110 — Wade McKoy
p. 111 (top) — Wade McKoy
p. 111 (bottom) — Florence McCall

Chapter Six
p. 113 — David Gonzales
p. 114 (top) — David Gonzales
p. 114 (bottom left) — Greg Von Doersten
p. 114 (bottom right) — Wade McKoy
p. 115 — Wade McKoy
p. 116 (top) — Greg Von Doersten
p. 116 (bottom) — Jonathan Selkowitz
p. 117 (top) — William Henry Jackson/Corbis
p. 117 (bottom) — Carl Oksanen
p. 118 — Wade McKoy
p. 119 (left) — Gene Downer collection
p. 119 (right) — Bettman/Corbis
p. 120 (left) — Jim Elder
p. 120 (right) — Bob Woodall
p. 121 (left) — Bob Woodall
p. 121 (right) — Courtesy of New Mobility Magazine

p. 122 — Roger Brown
p. 123 — Wade McKoy
p. 124 — Courtesy of Echo Film Productions
p. 125 — Bruce Morley
p. 126 — Bob Woodall
p. 127 (left) — Wade McKoy
p. 127 (top right) — Bob Woodall
p. 127 (bottom right) — David Gonzales
p. 128 — Bob Woodall
p. 129 — Wade McKoy
p. 130 — Chris Figenshau
p. 131 — Chris Figenshau
p. 132 — John Layshock
p. 133 — Jonathan Selkowitz
p. 134 — Greg Von Doersten
p. 135 — Carl Oksanen
p. 136 (left) — Greg Von Doersten
p. 137 (right) — Wade McKoy
p. 138 — Greg Von Doersten

Chapter Seven
p. 139 — Chris Figenshau
p. 140 — Greg Von Doersten
p. 141 — Fletcher Manley
p. 142 (left) — Chris Figenshau
p. 142 (right) — Jeff Diener
p. 143 (top) — David Gonzales
p. 143 (bottom) — Wade McKoy
p. 145 (top) — David Gonzales
p. 145 (bottom) — Wade McKoy
p. 146 — Wade McKoy
p. 147 — Wade McKoy
p. 148 — Chris Figenshau
p. 149 (both) — Wade McKoy/Bob Woodall
p. 150 — John Layshock
p. 151 — Chris Figenshau
p. 152 — Wade McKoy
p. 153 (both) — Wade McKoy
p. 154 — Wade McKoy
p. 155 — Wade McKoy

Chapter Eight
p. 157 — Greg Von Doersten
p. 158 (top) — Bob Woodall
p. 158 (bottom) — Carl Oksanen
p. 159 — Florence McCall
p. 160 (top) — Bob Woodall
p. 160 (bottom) — Florence McCall
p. 161 — Carl Oksanen
p. 162 (left) — David O'Connor
p. 163 — Carl Oksanen
p. 164 (both) — David Gonzales
p. 165 (top) — David Gonzales
p. 165 (bottom left) — Carl Oksanen
p. 165 (bottom right) — David Gonzales
p. 166 (left) — Jonathan Selkowitz
p. 166 (right) — Greg Von Doersten
p. 167 (left) — Jeff Diener
p. 167 (right) — Florence McCall
p. 168 (top) — Bob Woodall
p. 168 (bottom) — John Layshock
p. 169 (left) — Bob Woodall
p. 169 (right) — Bob Woodall
p. 170 — Jonathan Selkowitz
p. 171 (left) — Bob Woodall
p. 171 (right) — Jeff Diener

Last Tram
p. 172 (both) — David O'Connor/Jackson Hole Guide
p. 173 — David O'Connor/Jackson Hole Guide

Acknowledgments
p. 176 — David O'Connor/Jackson Hole Guide

Final Photo Spread
pp. 178, 179 — Wade McKoy